Bob Bondurant on
POLICE *and* PURSUIT DRIVING

D1558416

Bob Bondurant
and
Edwin J. Sanow

MBI Publishing Company

First published in 2000 by MBI Publishing Company, 729 Prospect Avenue, PO Box 1, Osceola, WI 54020-0001 USA

MBI Publishing Company books are also available at discounts in bulk quantity for industrial or sales-promotional use. For details write to Special Sales Manager at Motorbooks International Wholesalers & Distributors, 729 Prospect Avenue, Osceola, WI 54020-0001 USA.

Library of Congress Cataloging-in-Publication Data
Bob Bondurant on police & pursuit driving / Bob Bondurant & Ed Sanow.
    p. cm.
Includes index.
    ISBN 0-7603-0686-9 (paperback : alk. paper)
    1. Police pursuit driving. 2. Automobile driving—Safety measures. I. Title: Bob Bondurant on police and pursuit driving. II. Sanow, Edwin, J., III. Title.

On the front cover: Bob Bondurant began his racing career driving Corvettes in the 1950s, which eventually led him to a driver's seat on Carroll Shelby's Ford Cobra Team. He continued as a professional driver until retiring after a serious Can-Am accident in 1967. During his recovery, he formulated the plans for his driving school. In 1990, Bob Bondurant's dream of his own driving facility came true. The 1.6-mile road racing course at The Bondurant School near Phoenix includes courses for all age and driving groups that present every kind of curve and camber a racer or driver will ever find on the track or street. The School maintains a fleet of over 150 Ford Mustang Cobra Rs, Formula Fords, Mustang GTs, and Crown Victoria "Police Interceptors." *Greg Fresquez*

On the back cover: One of the many techniques taught by The Bondurant School is the "Straddle Technique." The half-lane straddle gives the officer a better view of what is ahead: both of traffic and obstacles. Not only is this an effective observation method, it can also have an intimidating affect on a fleeing motorist.

Edited by John Adams-Graf

Designed by Rebecca Allen

Printed in the United States of America

Contents

Acknowledgments

We'd like to thank the following individuals for their time, effort, and cooperation in helping us put together this book. Simply put, it couldn't have been done without them.

Lisa Allen, Director of Public Information, Maricopa County, Arizona, Sheriff's Department; Sheriff Joseph Arpaio, Maricopa County, Arizona; Deputy Steve Bakos, Maricopa County, Arizona; Raymond Beach, Michigan Law Enforcement Training Council, IADLEST; Corporal John Bellah, California State University, Long Beach Police; Lieutenant Joe Brugman, Chandler, Arizona, Police; BruceCameron, editor *Law and Order;* Officer Pat Farmer, Phoenix Police Academy; Lieutenant Dave Faulkner, Phoenix Police; Ford Motor Company and Special Vehicles Team; Greg Fresquez, Advertising and Public Relations Coordinator, The Bondurant School; Lieutenant Rusty Goodpastor, Indiana Law Enforcement Academy; Goodyear Tire and Rubber; Chief Eric Greenberg, Fowler, Indiana, Police; Captain KenGrogan, Hall County, Georgia, Sheriff's Department; Brent Halida, BSR chief driving instructor; Colonel Billy Hancock, Crisp County, Georgia Sheriff; Commissioner Maury Hannigan, California, Highway Patrol (retired); Sheriff Donnie Haralson, Crisp County, Georgia; Officer Rick Harbaugh, Phoenix Police; Officer Beth Hollick, Phoenix Police; Sergeant Larry Hollingsworth, California Highway Patrol; Chief Harold Hurtt, Phoenix Police; Deputy Marshal Rick Hutchison, Whitestown, Indiana, Police; Deputy Keith Jones, Marion County, Indiana; Charlie Jones, Bliss-Indiana Insurance, Inc.; Lieutenant John Keiper, Butler University (Indiana) Police; Gerald LaCrosse, The Desere' Foundation; Deputy Marshal Vince Lowe, Kentland, Indiana, Police; Philip Lynn, IACP National Law Enforcement Policy Center; Chan Martinez, Director of Sales and Marketing, The Bondurant School; Joseph McDowell, FLETC senior driving instructor; Sergeant Richard McLaughlin, Monroe County, Indiana, Sheriff's Department; Officer Anthony Meraz, Phoenix Police; Dianna Mich, Executive Assistant to Bob Bondurant; Lance Miller, National Law Enforcement & Corrections Tech Center; Pete Miller, Driving Instructor, The Bondurant School; Dave Moon, Hall County, Georgia, photographer; Earl R. Morris, Utah Comprehensive Emergency Management; Debi Mulford, Stop Stick, Inc.; Sergeant Charles Nutt, Georgia State Patrol; Deputy Dave Oberholtzer, Marion County, Indiana; Sergeant Ken Partain, Crisp County, Georgia; Ronnie Paynter, editor *Law Enforcement Technology;* Performance Friction, Inc.; Marshal Tim Piercy, Oxford, Indiana, Police; Dane Pitarresi, president, SkidCar USA; Joseph Potaczek, National Safety Council; Lieutenant Bill Reynolds, Chicago Police (Retired); Officer Greg Reynolds, Chicago Police; Matt Robertson, Driving Instructor, The Bondurant School; Patrick Sallaway, Driving Instructor, The Bondurant School; Officer Shawn Sallaway, Tucson, Arizona, Police; Captain Russ Schanlaub, Newton County, Indiana, Sheriff's Department; Rick Scuteri, Staff Photographer, The Bondurant School; Mike Speck, Driving Instructor, The Bondurant School; Deputy Marty Staford, Cook County, Georgia; Tomar Electronics, strobe lightbars, 800-338-3133 or www.tomar.com; Gary Uhte, president, Stop Stick, Inc.; Deputy Tom VanVleet, Newton County, Indiana; Kevin Weber, Driving Instructor, The Bondurant School; Allison Weis, Chandler, Arizona, Police; Sheriff Ernie Winchester, Benton County, Indiana; Thomas Witczak, Lakeshore Technical College; Deputy Mel Wright, Marion County, Indiana; Master Sergeant Steve Yenchko, Illinois State Police; Lieutenant Tim Young, Michigan State Police.

Foreword

Everyone knows that the job of a law enforcement officer is dangerous. Each day on television, in newspapers and magazines, there is an endless number of stories detailing the deadly encounters police officers and sheriff's deputies experience in the line of duty.

The drug-crazed dealer, the out-of-control spouse at the domestic violence call, and the gun-wielding criminal certainly pose monumental threats to law enforcement personnel. But what might surprise most of you is that these do not represent the most dangerous part of the job.

No, the single most dangerous thing facing deputies and police officers today is their patrol cars. Traffic accidents kill more deputies and officers each year than criminals. In fact, in the last 5 years throughout the United States, 218 police men and women were killed in traffic accidents while on duty. Since 1859, nearly 2,150 have died in work-related traffic accidents.

Statistics show us these tragedies happen all too often. This sheriff's office experienced the loss of a fine young deputy recently. He was on his way to a burglary call when his patrol car slammed into the side of a cement truck. Sadly, he was killed instantly—and needlessly.

That's why the best training available to teach law enforcement professionals the latest in advanced defensive driving techniques is so important to every sheriff's office and police department in our country.

That's why Bob Bondurant wrote this book.

Bob Bondurant is a main force in providing the finest instruction on advanced defensive police driving in the world. His reputation has earned him worldwide respect and renown. Police from all over the world come to him for the best training money can buy. They know, as we do here at the Maricopa County Sheriff's Office in Phoenix, Arizona, where The Bondurant School is headquartered, that there is no person better qualified to teach law enforcement officers how to stay alive in dangerous and difficult police situations that involve driving.

As the man known as the "Toughest Sheriff in America," I encourage every person in our field to read this book and then have his or her organization sign up the entire patrol force for the Bondurant training course. Doing so will save lives. Somewhere, someday, a wife or child, a parent or sister, a friend or partner will thank you for taking that step to protect a loved one from the most dangerous part of the job in law enforcement today.

—*Sheriff Joe Arpaio*
Maricopa County Sheriff's Office
Phoenix, Arizona

Preface

I began training law enforcement in 1969 at the Orange County Raceway with the Orange County Police Department. In 1970 The School moved to Ontario Motor Speedway where we trained the Ontario Police Department and many local departments including the Los Angeles Police Department and the Los Angeles County Sheriff's Department.

Both Los Angeles departments were very competitive with one another so what we did at the end was to put together a competition. It was a very close finish with the Los Angeles Police Department winning by approximately a tenth of a second. They were both very good under pressure.

We continued to train law enforcement when we moved up to Sears Point International Raceway in August 1973 including the San Francisco, the Oakland, and the Santa Rosa Police Department and the Forestry Service law enforcement people through the Santa Rosa criminal justice training center.

Currently, we train Maricopa County Sheriff's Department. Their instructors rent our facility and vehicles using one of our instructors for "quality control." The way we've organized the program with the Maricopa County Sheriff's Department works well for all of us. In fact, after a year of not participating in training with us they have found that all of the officers involved in accidents had not gone through our training. There were no accidents among those that had gone through the course. The statistics speak well for the training we provide.

We continue to train law enforcement personnel in our Executive Protection/Anti- Kidnapping course, our 4-Day Grand Prix Road Racing course and Advanced Racing courses. We train about 80% of the NASCAR stock car drivers at The School as well as some of the Indy car drivers. We also offer two- and three-day high performance courses and one- and two-day advanced teenage driving courses which have been quite successful. The teen courses, which we've been teaching for about twelve years help to change teens attitudes toward respecting their vehicles, respecting other drivers, learning car control techniques and respecting themselves by using what they've learned. We are very pleased with the excellent results from the teen courses.

Part of our growth is reflected in the budding Bondurant SuperKarts program. We use pro karts and twin engine karts which are non shifting, utilizing the same concepts of vehicle control, weight transfer, braking and smooth acceleration. What the karts teach is how to be quick, accurate, in control, smooth, and precise. The use of karts for training is substantially more cost-effective than using cars. The results are truly amazing.

I enjoyed co-writing with Ed Sanow. I would like to thank the people that helped us write this book including the Phoenix Police Department's Driving Academy, the Phoenix Police Department as well as the Chandler Police Department, Maricopa County Sheriff's Office and Dianna Mich for organizing, transposing and coordinating. It's been a pleasure to write this book on law enforcement driving and executive protection while reliving all of the training that we've done over the past 31 years. All of our instructors that teach the law enforcement program do an excellent job and I'm very proud of them.

I'd also like to thank Diana Mich, my executive assistant, Chan Martinez, our Director of Sales and Marketing, Greg Fresquez, our Advertising and Public Relations Coordinator, Rick Scuteri, our staff photographer, our shop, making sure the cars are in expert condition at all times, Ford Motor Company who builds the best performing cars for law enforcement, SVT, Lincoln-Mercury, Motorcraft/Quality Care and Visteon for great service and reliability, Goodyear for it's great tires with fantastic traction, smooth ride and predictable car control, Bell Sports for making motor racing safer each day, OMP for the best driving suits, gloves and shoes in racing, Recaro for the very best in seating, Texaco for the very best in high-performance fuel and lubrication, American Racing Wheels for strong and beautiful lightweight wheels, Eibach Springs and Monroe Shocks for the best in quality, Performance Friction, the makers of the best racing brakes in the world and the Tomar company for letting us use their light bars for our photo shoot.

I love what I do and have been teaching for 31 years. I'm pleased to be able to interact with the law enforcement community and those involved with executive protection driving. I hope you enjoy the book and get a lot out of it. If you'd like further information on The Bondurant School for High Performance Driving please give us a call at 1-800-842-RACE or write to us at P.O. Box 51980, Phoenix, AZ 85076-1980 or visit us on the Internet http://www.bondurant.com.

—Bob Bondurant

Introduction

Whether on routine patrol, responding to an emergency call, or pursuing a dangerous felon who needs to be caught before he or she harms others, driving skills are critical in the competent execution of a police officer's job. Combine good judgment, unwavering concentration, and top-flight performance driving skills, and any officer will be at the top of his or her profession. In this book, legendary race car driver Bob Bondurant and veteran Deputy Sheriff Ed Sanow combine skills for the definitive book on police driving.

First-rate enforcement driving skills allow an officer to use the performance abilities of the vehicle under all driving conditions and in all traffic situations. Very little skill is needed to simply floor the throttle and drive in a straight line. Performance driving involves what to do when it comes time to turn the steering wheel.

Starting with the basics of driving and vehicle handling, this book covers tips on the hour-by-hour, near-cruise control task of routine patrol, with one hand on the steering wheel and the other hand on the radar controller, MDT keypad, or holding a cup of coffee. It also discuss the advantages of ABS brakes, give tips for driving in adverse weather, and explain the emergency evasive driving techniques that must become almost instinctive reactions.

Emergency driving is different from routine patrol driving and from pursuit driving. Emergency driving is an urgent but solo response to a call. The officer runs Code 3/Signal 10 "lights and siren" and drives almost as hard as if he were in a pursuit. Bondurant and Sanow build on the basics of patrol driving with tips for high-speed cornering and correcting for both understeer and oversteer situations. The police-oriented "late apex" method of cornering is explained in detail, as are the mistakes of the "early apex" driving style.

With the foundation of high-speed driving laid, the racer and the deputy tackle the tough issue of pursuit driving: what to look for, squad car placement, how to keep up, how close to

get, when to call it off, how to force it to an end by rolling roadblocks, stationary roadblocks, and the PIT procedure.

Anyone with an interest in high-performance driving techniques will find this book useful. But police officers, who are involved in three times the number of accidents per million miles as the general public, may find it a lifesaver. Police officers from strictly urban areas have an accident rate almost six times that of the average motorist. Police officers, by the very nature of their job, need accident avoidance training more than other drivers.

Of the police officers who die in the line of duty, 49 percent are killed by gunfire. However, 38 percent, the second largest category, die as a result of a traffic accident: on routine patrol, during an emergency response, or while in pursuit.

One out of three pursuits initiated for traffic infractions ends in a collision. Two out of three pursuits initiated for felony reasons results in a collision. One out of eight pursuits ends in an injury to someone.

The high-speed pursuit is one of the most dangerous activities performed by a law enforcement officer. Pursuits should not be viewed as a challenge, as a race, or as a threat to ego. Instead, officers must view pursuits for exactly what they are: an extreme use of force involving a continuous series of life-and-death decisions that risk the life of the officer, the violator, occupants in the violator's vehicle, and dozens of innocent bystanders. There are no good pursuits. The best pursuit is no pursuit. The second-best pursuit is a short one.

All of the techniques in this book are based on courses taught at The Bondurant School, and all have real-world applications. The chapters are sprinkled with lessons learned on the street from officers all over America.

While the future of police pursuits may be uncertain, law enforcement officers will always need to drive hard and fast as they make emergency runs to Serve and Protect.

1

The Basics of Driving

All drivers, police officers included, have been taught to drive a car, but few drivers have had the opportunity to properly learn the true basics of driving. The real basics include the correct hand position, foot position, seating position, the use of eyes, and the importance of concentration.

Energy and Feeling

Sit up straight in your chair and put the balls of both feet on the floor. Keep reading the book. When you sit up straight, you will find that you are more alert. You can sense and feel better.

Energy starts at the base of the spine and travels up the back. The straighter the back, the quicker energy moves up the back to the neck to the brain. Keeping your feet flat on the floor gives more feeling in your feet. Slouch down again in your chair and continue reading—you are going to think and react more slowly because the spine has a curve in it now.

With the proper hand and foot positions and the proper seat back and steering wheel angles, the officer can sense and feel every move the police car makes.

As a car passes over the road, it's possible to sense and feel every move it makes. You can feel it up through the tire patches, front tires, suspension, steering column, steering hub of the wheel, and out to the spokes. You can feel messages through your feet on the pedals. Vibrations sent through the chassis are transferred through the seat rails and seat. These seat-of-the-pants messages are relayed by the car seat to your legs, lower back, and upper back. You can feel them through your shoulders, arms, wrists, and palms of your hands on the steering wheel. Use your thumbs to rest, not hang, on the spokes of the steering wheel, and let your entire body sense and feel what the car is doing at all times. You want to be one with the car, to sense and feel every move the car makes at all times.

Visualize yourself driving a police car. Put your hands up just as if you were holding onto the steering wheel. Place your hands to what would be equivalent to the 3 o'clock and the 9 o'clock positions. Keep your arms flexed so that you can maneuver the wheel all the way to the left or all the way to the right.

Imagine you are in a lights-and-siren pursuit. Your hands and body will tighten up the faster you go, especially when driving over your head, because the body senses every move you make. When the body is doing something it doesn't want to do, it tightens up. Your arms and hands are going to tense and tighten up. As soon as your hands tighten up, they lose about 50 percent of their feel. Feel is control. If someone pulls out in front of you, you may react too slowly to avoid the collision or lose control of your car attempting to swerve.

In this situation, you want to back off your speed to the point you feel comfortable, confident, and in control again. Remain alert, right on top of everything: looking, sensing, feeling every move that the car makes. Look for areas where you know you'll find traffic—the side streets, driveways, intersections, etc.

Hand Position

While other schools teach the steering wheel "hand shuffle," the "hand-over" and "palm-over" techniques are faster and more

For optimum control and smooth steering inputs, the proper steering wheel hand position puts the left hand at 9 o'clock and the right hand at 3 o'clock. *Rick Scuteri*

precise. The Bondurant School teaches the "hand-over" technique. The pressure exerted by the hands is as important as hand position. The thumbs and palms should exert heavier pressure while the fingers should exert lighter pressure.

Say you need to turn left. To use the "hand-over" technique, take your left hand (the 9 o'clock position) off the steering wheel while still going in a straight line. Reach over and grasp the right side of the steering wheel near the right hand (the 3 o'clock position). Grasp and pull with the left hand while relaxing the grip with your right hand. You can easily turn the steering wheel a half-turn, or 180 degrees, with two hands on the wheel and in full control.

Most turns, corners, intersections, and lane changes can be negotiated by turning the wheel less than a half-turn. The 3 and 9 hand position allows the wheel to turn up to a half-turn without changing hand positions.

As the steering wheel continues around to 180 degrees, you can continue to turn the wheel. If the corner requires more steering input, you can not continue to turn the

Bondurant teaches the "hand-over" steering method for both routine and emergency response driving. To make a right turn, with the hands at the 3 and 9 position, the right hand comes over to meet the left hand. As the wheel is turned right, the left hand relaxes the grip. *Rick Scuteri*

The 3 and 9 position allows a half-turn of the wheel without changing hand positions. If the corner requires more steering input, you can continue to move your "hands-over" in the direction of the turn. Thanks to Ackerman steering geometry, most corners and intersections can be negotiated with just one hand movement. *Rick Scuteri*

wheel a full 360 degrees, one full turn, without changing your hand position again.

As you come out of the turn, simply reverse the procedure. Unwind the wheel a half-turn, slide your right hand to meet your left hand, pull the wheel through with your right hand while releasing your left hand grip on the wheel. This method allows you to be very smooth with the steering wheel. It also minimizes having to take your hands off the wheel while turning in and turning out of the corner.

The proper hand position for routine patrol driving may be different than the proper hand position for enforcement and pursuit driving. The 3 and 9 position should be used as often as possible. However, hand positions

that work for a 30-minute pursuit or road race may be too fatiguing for a 10-hour patrol shift.

Instead, one-hand driving is common for routine patrol. One-hand driving is also necessary when the officer is using the other hand to operate the radio, activate the instant-on radar, turn on the in-car video, or key in data into the MDT. However, the officer must be able to rapidly return to the 3 and 9 position. The proper one-hand position is the left hand at the 9 o'clock position. This allows the right hand to operate the police equipment and still return immediately to the 3 o'clock position for best performance. The 12 o'clock position should not be used.

In the "hand shuffle" technique, the hands never cross over each other. Instead,

The 3 and 9 hand position may be better for use during routine patrol and emergency response. The "hand shuffle" technique may be better during a pursuit, when the microphone is frequently held in the right hand.

One-hand driving is common for routine patrol when the other hand is busy, operating instant-on radar, for example. Keep the left hand at 9 o'clock. The right hand can quickly return to the 3 o'clock position.

The proper seat back to steering wheel distance allows the wrist to just drop over the rim of the wheel. The wheel should be at a 30-degree angle while the seat back should be nearly upright.

Don't use your left foot to brake! Your right foot is more control sensitive and allows you to be smoother. In some panic stops, the left-foot braker will end up pressing down on both the gas and brakes.

the wheel slides through your hands. For example, with your hands starting in the 4 and 8 o'clock positions, to turn left you loosen the grip of the left hand, turn the wheel with the right until your hands meet, then re-grip with the left hand and continue turning as the right hand loosens its grip and the wheel slides through it. As the steering wheel continues around to the left 180 degrees, you must slide the left hand up to 12 o'clock, thereby being able to turn the wheels without crossing your hands and running out of turning capability. Reverse the procedure to come out of the turn.

The 3 and 9 hand position may be better for use during an emergency response to a call, while the hand shuffle technique may be better for use during a pursuit when a mike is held in one hand.

Seating Position

The steering wheel should be adjusted to about a 30-degree angle. To help you sense and feel what the car is doing, remember to sit up straight in the car. Adjust the seatback almost upright. The correct basic seating position is sitting upright, feet on the floorboard.

To get the proper arm-to-wheel distance, with your shoulders against the seat back, stretch out either your left or right arm so your wrist is on top of the steering wheel and your hand just drops over the wheel. This is the perfect arm position—you are neither too close nor too far away from the wheel. If you are too far away, you will pull your shoulders off the seat back as your hands follow the arc of the wheel. If you are too close, your arms will get locked and tangled as the wheel is turned. With the proper distance from the wheel, you can quickly maneuver in an emergency. The proper leg position has your leg still slightly bent under the most extreme application of the gas and brake pedal. Your leg should be able to push both pedals to the floor without locking straight at the knees. Simply adjust the seat position so your legs are slightly bent at the full length of pedal travel; too close, and you will not be able to move between the pedals smoothly, too far, and you will not be able to fully depress the pedals. More specifically, you will not be able to adjust braking pressure as precisely if your leg is fully extended.

Foot Position and Braking

When driving a patrol car with an automatic transmission, use your right foot to

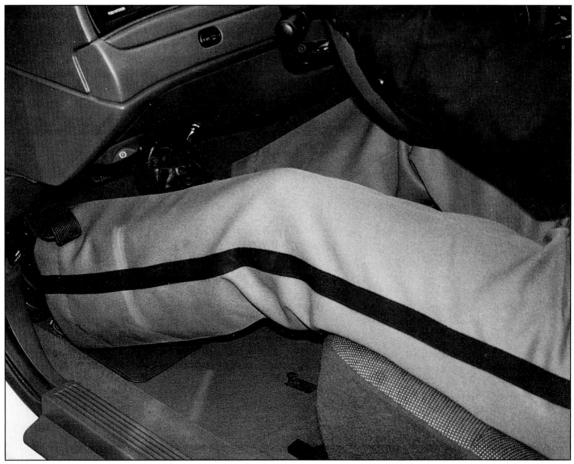

The proper position for the left foot is on the "dead pedal" to the far left of the floorboard. Use the left foot to brace yourself in a nice three-point suspension.

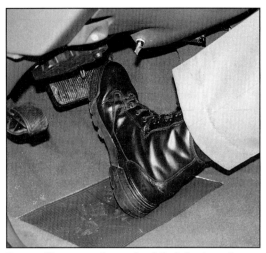

Some officers use the arch of their foot on the brake pedal, which leaves their heel in the air. Much greater braking precision comes from using the ball of the foot on the pedal, pivoting off the heel on the floorboard.

brake. Most drivers have more sensitivity and feel in their right foot than their left foot because of years of using their right foot to precisely modulate the accelerator. If you've been using your left foot to brake for a long time and have as much sensitivity and feel as in your right foot and feel comfortable doing it, left-foot braking is acceptable, but still not recommended.

You can teach yourself left-foot braking, but when you get into a panic situation, your left foot will slam on the brakes instead of squeeze on the brakes. On a non-ABS car, this will lock up the brakes. On a car with ABS, this will overapply the brakes. You will brake too hard or too abruptly.

It is easier to be smooth in rolling off the gas and squeezing on the brakes if the right foot is used to do both. The time it takes the right foot to move from the gas pedal to the brake pedal is not wasted. In fact, it allows time for the suspension to get set during the transition. The rapid and abrupt change from gas off to brakes on that often comes when left-foot braking upsets the suspension and weight transfer.

Left-foot braking also gets the car working against itself as the gas and brake pedals are frequently pressed, at least a little bit, at

the same time. In some panic situations, both are floor-boarded at the same time. In nearly all driving with left-foot braking, there is a loss of smoothness in the transition from gas to brakes to gas. In an emergency stop, the "left-foot braker" can end up with both the accelerator and brake pedal depressed. Not only is the engine trying to keep the car moving, but vacuum boost is reduced and more pedal pressure is required to operate the brakes. Another problem with left-foot braking is that the steering wheel becomes a handle to hang on to, rather than a device to steer the car.

A driver is best braced when the left foot is placed against the left floorboard of the car and the right foot is positioned over the accelerator pedal. The three-point suspension provided will stabilize the driver's position behind the steering wheel and help retain control during sudden vehicle movements that occur during an evasive action, mechanical failure, or actual impact with another object. The proper place for your left foot is on the floorboard, at the far left side, on the "dead-pedal," to help hold yourself in place.

Many officers brake with the arch of their foot and their heel in the air. A more precise way to brake is with the ball of the foot on the pedal and the heel on the floorboard. With this method, the ball of the foot pivots off the heel. The brake pressure comes from the calf muscle. With the heel off the floor, the brake pressure comes from the thigh muscle. The calf muscle and ankle pivot work together to produce more precise brake pressure changes than the thigh muscle.

Proper braking is much more related to precise pedal pressure than to coarse or sheer pedal pressure. Today's power brakes don't require a heavy pedal effort, as much as they do require a *controlled* pedal effort. Small changes in pedal pressure produce big changes in braking force. Try it both ways. You will find you are smoother and have more control if you pivot off your heel.

Look Where You Want To Go

Learn how to use your eyes. Look ahead as far as you can see. Then come back to the mirrors: outside left, inside rear, and outside right. Immediately look

Use your mirrors! Get in the habit of a visual rotation sequence. Every few seconds look in the left outside mirror, the inside rear view mirror, and the right outside mirror. If you have to make an evasive maneuver, you will know where the open lanes are without delay.

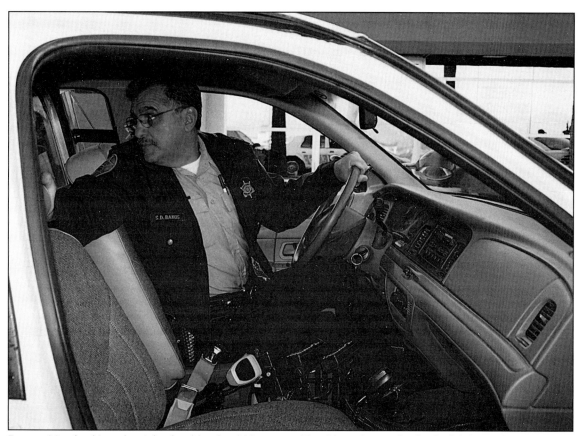

For precision backing, the right shoulder should be pressed hard into the seat back. The left hand should be at the 12 o'clock position. That way, the officer can feel when the wheel is centered without looking at the wheel.

through the car ahead of you to see if the driver is paying attention. Many drivers lack concentration. Constantly move your eyes to see where traffic is around you. Check out every intersection, even when you're using emergency equipment. Most drivers will not hear the siren or notice the lights in time.

When on the street, you have vehicles coming from every direction and you can't count on people doing the right thing at the right time. In fact, expect them to do the wrong thing all the time. That is the essence of defensive driving.

Look far ahead of your car. Time and again, it has been proven at The Bondurant School that you will drive exactly where you are looking. Look as far around a corner as you can, 10 to 15 car-lengths, if possible. Don't over-drive your vision. Look where you want to be.

Tests have revealed that most drivers do not look far enough ahead. The faster we drive, the farther ahead we should look. The officer must make a conscious effort to raise the visual horizon. Many drivers were taught in driver education to focus on the hood ornament. They were told to place the hood ornament at a certain spot relative to the shoulder of the road to help keep them in the middle of their driving lane. Unfortunately, this technique is wrong because it teaches the driver to look at the hood of the car instead of the horizon of the road.

Look as far ahead as possible, or at least one block ahead in city traffic. The purpose is to keep the driver's view "up" rather than looking "down" at the area in front of the car. Keep your eyes moving. Establish a visual search pattern. Look near and far, to the left and right, in the mirrors, and at the instrument panel. Get the big picture. Become aware of the whole traffic flow around you.

Scan curves as far ahead as possible and mentally plot the line you are going to take before you get there. If you can't see ahead around a curve, reduce your speed. Looking far enough ahead is the single, most important factor in attaining smoothness in the control of your vehicle.

The key to performance driving is to look where you want to go. This is especially true of skid control or obstacle avoidance. Don't look at the obstacle or you will certainly drive right into it. Instead, look at where your escape route is. In a slide, look to where you want the car to be as you recover from the slide.

Wear your seat belt! It takes less than three seconds to fasten and can be unfastened before you brake to a stop on a routine traffic stop. The air bag only works as designed if the occupant is belted in place. Seat belts hold you in place during aggressive driving.

Suppose you are sliding toward a parked car. The tendency is to look toward that parked car. Instead, move your eyes back to where you are trying to go. Believe it or not, the instinctive eye-hand coordination will steer you back out of that skid. The same is true for sliding into a telephone pole, a tree, or any obstacle. Most of us fixate on the pole or tree we are about to hit and forget about where we want to go. Force yourself by training to look where you want the car to go.

One of the best ways to do this in training is to set up a tall pylon. Put yourself in a slide toward it; look at it while trying to correct for the slide. You will find you run right over it. Next time look beyond it, look back on the road where you want to go, and you will find yourself steering right out of the slide.

The Importance of Concentration

When you're driving the car, be it your patrol car or your personal car, part of concentration is making sure you're looking down the road well ahead. Remember that you will drive exactly where you're looking. Your hands will follow your eyes. To concentrate on your driving just simply pay attention to where you are going. Look at least 15 to 20 car lengths ahead. Then come back and look through all three mirrors, and then go back to the cars that are just ahead to see if those drivers are looking ahead. Or are they not concentrating by talking on the phone or interacting with their passengers? You want to be looking ahead, concentrating on what's in front of you. What's coming out of the side streets? Is someone starting to get into an accident ahead, is traffic starting to slow down ahead of you? If so, ease off on the gas and be ready to make an emergency lane change. Concentration is really looking ahead and paying attention to what is going on around you. It's as simple as that.

A Word on Seat Belts

Some law enforcement officers do not use seat belts when driving their police cruisers. This is a potentially fatal mistake. Some reasons given for not wearing seat belts include low speeds during routine patrol; yet more than 80 percent of all accidents occur at speeds less than 40 miles per hour. Other reasons include short trips taken by many officers responding to a call; yet 75 percent of all accidents happen within 25 miles of home, or the fear of entrapment in the event of an accident; yet less than one-half of one percent of all injury-producing collisions involve fire or submersions. Too time consuming? It takes under three seconds to fasten a combination lap and shoulder harness.

Many good reasons exist for wearing safety belts. They protect the wearer from a "secondary collision." The car strikes an object (primary collision), and at the same speed the driver strikes the steering wheel or windshield (secondary collision). A driver wearing a seat belt has a "safety zone" between himself and the vehicle.

Seat belts prevent occupants from hitting one another during a collision. Seat belts diffuse and spread out the force of the impact across the strong parts of the body, hips, and shoulders. Seat belts prevent the driver from being ejected in the event of a collision or roll-over accident. Police officers, more than any other drivers, know the safest place for the driver is inside the car. From a driving performance view, the seat belt holds the driver in position for best control during aggressive driving.

Wear the seat belt and shoulder harness all the time. Some officers do not wear seat belts, thinking seat belts will get in the way of a fast exit on a felony stop. Felony stops are rare. This is no excuse for not wearing seatbelts during the multiple dozens of stops a traffic officer makes each day. A felony stop may be just the kind you need your seat belt for, if the violator uses his vehicle to ram or otherwise forcibly resist. On a felony stop, unbelt just before your cruiser comes to a stop.

If you are counting on the air bag, you had better have your seat belt on every time you drive. If you don't have your seat belt on and get hit head-on, your body can slide underneath the steering wheel. The steering wheel can go right into your chest or your face. Protect yourself. Wear your seat belt.

2

The Basics of Handling

Vehicle control is directly related to tire traction, which is directly related to tire patch size, weight transfer, and smoothness. Learning to be smooth with your input to steering, acceleration, and braking is critical to maximizing control of your vehicle.

Steering Geometry

The idea of steering the front wheels around separate axes was invented in 1817 by a carriage builder in Munich, Germany, named Lankensperger. In 1878, French carriage builder Charles Jeantaud introduced a refinement known as the "Jeantaud Diagram"

Everyone who has been through The Bondurant School remembers THE VAN RIDE. Bob Bondurant opens up each School course with some hot laps in a 15-passenger van. The point is made forever: the basics of handling are the same for race cars and for police interceptors as they are for all vehicles. *Rick Scuteri*

that provided a more precise prediction of the correct front suspension geometry. Today, Lankensperger's invention, along with Jeantaud's refinements, is referred to as "Ackerman Steering" and is designed into every vehicle, including police cars, vans, trucks, buses, race cars, or go 'karts.'

The Ackerman suspension is designed so that the inside wheel turns in at more of an angle than the outside wheel. This helps to pull the car into and through a corner. If both wheels turned in exactly the same amount in response to the steering wheel, the car would tend to push to the outside of the corner. The Ackerman designed into the steering helps steer the car to the inside of the corner.

To make a change from one lane to another, you only need to turn the steering wheel slightly. Hands that were at the 3 and 9 position only need to turn the steering wheel to where the hands are now at the 2 and 8 position. Believe it or not, you can make a lane change without even a quarter of a turn of the steering wheel.

Just for a drill, go out to your car, and turn the steering wheel just slightly, until

As you accelerate, brake, and corner, weight shifts back and forth and from side to side. Literally all aspects of vehicle dynamics get back to the issue of weight transfer. The key to vehicle control is to transfer weight to the area of the car needing traction respectively. *Rick Scuteri*

When the car is at rest, depending on the weight distribution and tire size, all four tire patches are about the same size. Each patch is about the size of a man's palm. These small patches are all you have between control and loss of control.

As you lift off the gas, weight transfers from the rear to the front, making the front tire patches larger. As you apply the brakes, a great deal of weight transfers forward, making the front patches very large and the rear patches very small. The opposite happens as you ease off the brakes and apply full throttle.

Here is the car at rest with nearly equal weight on all four tires. As you enter a turn, weight shifts from the inside tires to the outside tires. *Smoothly* turning the steering wheel *smoothly* transfers weight and maintains control.

your 3 and 9 hand position is at the 2 and 8 position. Get out of the car and look how little the tires have moved. They will have barely turned. To make an emergency lane change at highway speeds, it only takes about an eighth- or quarter-turn of the steering wheel. Get back in the car and turn the steering wheel a total of a half-turn. Get back out and look at how much the inside wheel has turned now. You will find it is turned in more.

Turn the steering wheel a total of one turn, as if you are making a panic lane change. If you yank the wheel in a panic, you can turn almost a full turn of the steering wheel. Now get out and look at the front wheels. The inside front wheel will have turned in a lot more. The more you turn the steering wheel, the more the inside wheel is

going to turn for you. And if you turn it way too far, you will overcorrect, upsetting the balance of the car, and you will likely lose control of the car. If you use 3 and 9 all the time, you can not overcorrect the steering in an emergency situation. This is one of the reasons this hand position is so important.

Weight Transfer and Traction

Car control is a matter of controlling the weight transfer and tire patch sizes, because this is what controls traction and tire adhesion. You control the amount of traction during acceleration, braking, and cornering by controlling the size of the tire patches.

Every time you drive the police car, you induce weight transfer. When the car is at rest, and depending on the weight distribution and the tire size, all four tire patches

Here is the same police car going around a curve at maximum adhesion. Even the stiffly sprung Ford Police Interceptor has rolled slightly to the outside. A great deal of weight is on the outside front tire. Note how much the tire is rolled under, compared to the car at rest.

are about the same size. As soon as you start to accelerate, weight shifts from the front to the rear. The front end has less weight and the front tires have smaller tire patches. A smaller tire patch means less traction. The weight will transfer more to the rear of the car, compressing the rear springs, pushing down on the rear tires making a larger tire patch. A larger tire patch results in more traction and stability.

The same kind of weight transfer happens as the steering wheel is turned. In a right hand turn, weight transfers to the left, causing the front and rear left side tire patches to grow, and the front and rear right side patches to shrink.

Between you and the road are four tire patches about the size of the palm on a man's hand. That is all you have between you and the road, between you and traction, between you being in control or out of control.

In a panic, drivers often lift off the gas and turn the wheel quickly. When this happens, the weight transfers forward onto the front tires. By compressing the front springs downward, you have a larger tire patch which means better traction on the front. However, the rear tires have much less traction, because weight has transferred away from the rear and the rear springs have released their downforce. The rear tire patches are now half the size.

Lifting off the gas and jerking the steering wheel is usually followed by jumping on the brakes and braking as hard as you can. On a car without ABS (one police cruiser out of four still does not have ABS) this action will lock up the front wheels. With the front wheels locked and the rear wheels with so little traction, the rear end will just spin right around. You now have spun out of control and perhaps hit something else, trying to avoid the first object.

As the car negotiates a corner, it rolls to the outside, transferring weight. Vehicle control is related to traction, tire patch size, weight transfer, and smoothness.

Go back to the 3 and 9 hand position. The 3 and 9 hand position will not allow you to overcorrect the steering wheel. You are going down the highway and someone suddenly stops in your lane. Lift off the gas, but don't touch the brakes. Turn the steering wheel a quick half-turn. As you're crossing over the white line into the other lane, simply squeeze on the gas again. This transfers weight back to the rear wheels to maintain traction. You will be by the situation much quicker and safer than if you tried to brake.

Try this demonstration with a friend. Have him put his arm out straight, palm up. Put your arm out, palm down on top of his hand. Push down slightly on his hand like the pressure on the front springs during braking. Have him push up slightly, just enough to counteract the pressure. Now, suddenly lift your hands, which will remove the downward pressure. Your friend's arm will suddenly pop up into the air. Springs and the whole concept of weight transfer work the same way. When you suddenly accelerate, the front springs release their downforce. The front tire patches rapidly decrease in size.

If you treat the accelerator as if it were a sponge, apply pressure as if you were squeezing water out of it. Squeeze on the throttle smoothly, you will always have smooth weight transfer under acceleration.

To begin braking, roll smoothly off the gas pedal and squeeze smoothly on the brakes. Treat the brake pedal like the accelerator, as if it were a sponge. If you are smooth on the brakes, you will transfer weight forward onto the front tires while still maintaining some tire patch, which means traction, on the rear wheels.

The way humans react, if you lift off the gas rapidly, you will also hit the brake hard. If you roll off the gas smoothly, you will also squeeze the brakes smoothly. When you do that, you will control the weight transfer smoothly and always have traction on all four wheels. That is the key to being in control.

When you accelerate, the weight transfers to the rear of the car, taking weight off the front. What that means is, the rear shocks are compressed, expanding the rear tire patches. While that is happening, the front springs are releasing their downforce. How hard you accelerate or how smoothly you accelerate governs how much traction you have in the rear and how much traction you lose in the front.

When coming down the road at 40 or 50 miles per hour and you are going to brake, you ease off the gas, and the weight starts to transfer forward; follow that by smoothly squeezing on the brake pedal, transferring more weight to the front, maintaining some rear tire patch while you expand the front tire patches. This maintains traction front and rear.

Weight Transfer and Cornering

When braking and turning into a corner, the car's weight transfers to the outside and front while the brakes are applied. Then when you accelerate through the corner, weight transfers to the outside and rear of the car, expanding the rear tire patches and taking away the front traction or tire patches, depending on how hard you accelerate.

When you make a turn under acceleration, weight will transfer to the outside rear wheel, providing traction there. The inside front wheel has less traction. Consequently, if you accelerate too hard through a corner, the front end is going to push. It is going to understeer, which is a front-wheel slide. To get out of that situation, roll the throttle back on. Weight will transfer forward and put downforce on the tire patches through the springs. The sidewall will also deflect and scrub off speed for you.

It is not necessary to brake. However, if you are understeering and you don't gain front tire traction quickly enough, gently squeeze the brakes to transfer more weight forward and regain front tire traction again.

Say you are coming into a right-hand corner, and you have jumped on the brakes too hard. Under hard braking and hard cornering, the weight will transfer laterally from right to left and longitudinally from the rear to the front. It takes weight off the right rear tire, resulting in a smaller tire patch and less traction. It transfers weight to the left front tire, resulting in a larger tire patch and more traction. However, the right front tire also has good traction because

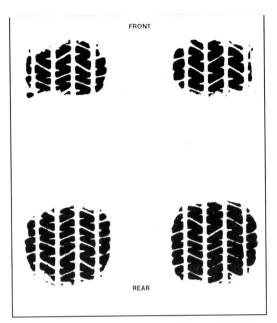

These images of tire contact patches are ideal for showing the actual effects of weight transfer on your car. This will vary slightly with the size and type of tire as well as the car, but in concept it can be used for a base of reference. These examples are from a Formula Ford, as the rear tires are larger than the front tires. This shows the car at rest.

braking has shifted the weight forward. The result of all this weight transfer is the back end can start to slide out.

To correct for the rear wheel slide, called oversteer, as quickly as you can, turn the wheel to the left to stabilize the car. The tires again are going to scrub off speed. If it is not enough correction, squeeze on the gas a little to put weight back on the rear tires. Carry the slide through the corner, nice and smooth. If you jump on the brakes in the middle of a rear-wheel slide, you are going to make the weight transfer problem worse and are going to spin the car out.

Lateral Weight Transfer

All aspects of vehicle dynamics get back to the issue of weight transfer. The key to vehicle control is simply to transfer weight to the area of the car needing traction.

When a car is turned right or left from its course of travel, a lateral weight transfer occurs. This causes the suspension to be compressed on one side and expanded on the opposite side. Normally, the curve is completed and the vehicle's chassis returns to lateral neutral. However, if the vehicle is immediately turned in the opposite direction, this energy stored

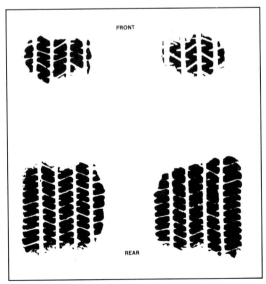

Under acceleration the front patch has changed little—but look at the tremendous difference in the rear imprints as the weight transfers rearward.

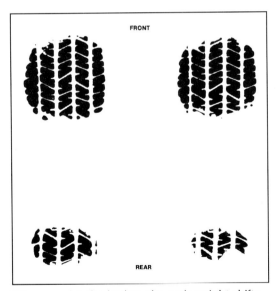

When you hit the brakes, the car's weight shifts dramatically toward the front.

The next three images show how the tire contact patches change through a right-hand corner. Lateral weight transfer in a corner is pronounced. Note that even within the left front tire patch itself, the outside (left) edge is being forced into the pavement more than the inside edge of the tread.

In the middle of the corner, the tire patches show a further lightening of both the front and rear inside (right) tires.

in the suspension can induce a violent lateral weight transfer.

When negotiating a series of reversing turns, these weight transfers can have a cumulative effect. Each lateral transfer becomes more violent than the one preceding it. If this keeps going, the vehicle will spin out of control. A driver must consider what reaction the vehicle will have to the driver's action. Smoothness in steering, braking, and throttle is the only effective way to minimize lateral weight transfers.

Tires can only perform at their maximum when doing one thing at a time. You can only corner at maximum adhesion or accelerate at maximum adhesion or brake at maximum adhesion. If you try to turn while braking at the maximum, the front tires will almost certainly slide or the front brakes lock. If you try to turn while accelerating at the maximum, the rear tires will almost certainly slide or start spinning. If you try to brake or accelerate while turning at the maximum, the front tires will slide (understeer), the rear tires will slide

As progress is made to the exit of the corner, all four patches begin to show weight transfer back to a more stable position.

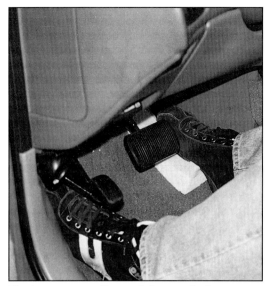

The key to controlling weight transfer is to smoothly apply the gas. Imagine a big sponge under the gas pedal. Squeeze on the gas like squeezing water out of a sponge. Squeeze on. Ease off.

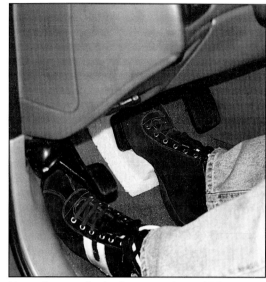

Never jam on the brakes, even in an ABS-equipped car. Instead, smoothly transfer weight forward when braking. Imagine a huge sponge is below the brake pedal. Squeeze on. Ease off.

(oversteer), or all four tires will slide (four-wheel drift).

Weight transfer, tire patches, and Ackerman steering geometry all go together. The tire patch is where the tire meets the asphalt. Tire patch is about the size of the palm of your hand. When sitting still, all four tire patches are about the same. As you accelerate, weight transfers to the rear, and compresses the rear springs, pressing down on the rear tire patch making it larger. At the same time that is happening, front tire patches are becoming smaller. As weight transfers to the rear, it releases pressure on the front springs, which moves weight upward and backward.

As you approach a corner and roll off the gas, weight starts to transfer forward, and next you squeeze on the brakes. All forward motion compresses downward on the front tire patches, making them larger and larger, making rear tires patches smaller and smaller. As long as you let off the gas and brake smoothly, you will always have all four tire patches working for you.

As soon as you start to turn into a corner, say a left-hand corner, the weight will transfer laterally across from left rear to right front, putting more weight on the front tire, creating more of a tire patch. The Ackerman steering takes over. The more you turn the wheel, the tighter Ackerman turns, and helps to steer you into the corner. One problem to keep in mind is if you turn the wheel suddenly to full lock, it is going to turn the outside front tire past the area of rolling friction. Tire patch size won't help the problem either. You will have to unwind the wheel a little bit to have rolling friction.

When you're smoothly on the gas, the brakes, and the steering wheel, weight will transfer between all four wheels. This means the total traction and adhesion of the car will be greater than if you were rougher with the gas, brakes, and wheel. Vehicle control is directly related to tire traction, which is directly related to tire patch size, weight transfer, and smoothness.

3

The Right
Mental Attitude

No matter what we do in life, to do it well, we must concentrate on it. We must put our minds to it, and work to accomplish it. Driving takes more concentration than most drivers realize. Enforcement driving, like race car driving, requires the maximum possible concentration.

A key difference exists between an advanced driver and a beginning driver. The beginning driver does the basics right some of the time, while the advanced driver does the basics right all of the time. More than training and experience, the true difference between the beginning and the advanced driver is actually concentration.

Concentrate on driving 100 percent of the time. It can be done. Nearly every accident is avoidable. It is called an accident because someone does not pay attention. That someone was not concentrating.

Most people don't concentrate when they drive. They pay attention perhaps 30 percent of the time. Most drivers think driving is a natural activity. Like it's a freebie. Anyone can drive a car. They don't control the car; it controls them. They don't look far enough ahead. They don't concentrate at all. They don't pay attention to what other drivers are doing around them. They just cruise around listening to the radio, thinking about where they are going, what they are going to be doing that night, their next meeting, their next meal. This happens to police officers, too.

You are patrolling, but not paying a lot of attention to what your car is doing: not looking for a car coming out of a driveway, or an alley way, or turning right on red, or making a left turn across oncoming traffic. You can get into trouble just as easily as anyone else driving a car. If you concentrate, you can stay out of trouble. For police officers concentration is doubly important. They are not only driving but also patrolling the streets. Unlike regular drivers, their job is to watch for things that have nothing to do with driving.

Whether you are driving a Formula Ford, a Mustang Cobra, or a Police Interceptor, the key to successful driving is maximum concentration. Concentration is the key to both accident avoidance and smoothness.

Concentrating on enforcement driving is not just staring down the road. It is looking far ahead and anticipating what traffic will do. Good visual habits allow the officer to resist distractions.

The Mental Approach to Pursuit

I did a training exercise at the Phoenix Police Academy, and right away they put me in a chase. I was the bad guy, and then I was the good guy. Once again, concentration is the most important thing that needs to be emphasized in pursuit driving. Focus on driving your own line. It is easy to be chasing someone, and all of a sudden they make a mistake. You follow that mistake. You both crash.

I was chasing their chief instructor. I caught him, and I stayed about three car lengths behind. After what happened next, in retrospect, I was probably a little bit close. I watched his driving and saw he was getting wide on the corners. The back end was sliding out. He just got carried away trying to elude me. Finally, he spun out. I pushed the car to the limit to avoid making contact with him. As close as I was behind him, I could see how easy it would be to just follow his line. In fact, it was very hard not to follow his lead. I concentrated on following my own line rather than concentrating on him. It was easy to catch him that way.

During a pursuit you must try extra hard to drive your own line into the corners. He will turn into the corner too soon, too early, and cut the corner. This is called an early apex. You must stay to the outside and wait longer before turning in. This is taking a late apex. He will brake too late. You must brake early.

Most of all, back off and give the fleeing driver room. You will find yourself gaining on the driver as he makes mistakes and you don't. You must concentrate on keeping the same gap. You will actually find yourself waiting on the fleeing driver, under-driving your car, accelerating less than it is capable, and braking less aggressively. Simply put, your more conservative line is allowing you to catch the fleeing driver. At the most extreme, with your 215-horsepower four-door sedan versus his 330-horsepower sports car, you will be able to keep up with him. This is because you are doing a better job of technical driving where you would otherwise be easily outrun.

Remember, it's not a game of tag. All you need to do is keep him in sight. If you get too close, you will start to follow his braking and cornering mistakes and you will both crash. Backing off allows you the mental flexibility to drive correctly.

Sometimes the best decision during a pursuit is to be patient, to feel that you don't necessarily have to "get" an alleged offender right now. It might be better to either get the license number and find the driver later, or wait until he or she makes a mistake. Patience involves your ability to look at an emergency situation logically and objectively, not emotionally and subjectively.

—Bob Bondurant

Perhaps one reason that so many accidents happen under "safe" driving conditions is that these are the times when the average driver is easily distracted. Over 70 percent of all accidents occur in moderate traffic, on straight roads, during dry and clear weather conditions.

Nine out of 10 motorists show by their actions in traffic that they do not use their eyes correctly while driving. A major difference between the average motorist and a good police driver is that common distractions or other adverse conditions do not lower the ability of the police driver as much as they do a less-skillful driver.

The high incidence of serious single-car accidents is proof that many individual drivers make serious driving errors that could be avoided by better visual habits. As a driver, these seeing habits will enable you to pay attention to key details, resist distractions, and allow sufficient time and space to adjust safety to traffic situations.

Look and Anticipate

Concentrating is not just staring down the road. It is looking way ahead and anticipating what the traffic will do. Look as far down the road as you can. Then come back and look through the mirrors—all three mirrors, so you know where traffic is around your vehicle. Then look into the car ahead. What is that driver doing? Is he talking on a cell phone or talking so much to his passengers that he is not paying attention? The distracted driver may suddenly see your police car in the rearview mirror, think he is going to get a ticket, and suddenly jump on the brakes or do something else stupid. You must be ready for that. Just as you are taught by every other police instructor: Expect the unexpected.

At The Bondurant School, we have done various tests in the past. With a police officer behind me, the agreement was I would slow down only when I heard the siren. If the driver is staring down the road

The average motorist will not see your flashing emergency lights nor hear your siren until it is too late. The police officer must drive defensively and expect the unexpected. *Ford Division*

The police officer must take in an incredible amount of information in an ever-changing environment. Concentration on the task is critical. Successful police enforcement driving is 10 percent physical and 90 percent mental. *Ford Division*

and not paying attention, he may not see the emergency lights, even if the officer is right behind the offender. This is especially the case when the driver thinks he is driving in an acceptable manner and is not expecting to see a police officer. If the driver has the radio on, the windows up, and the air conditioning on, we have found he will not hear the siren until the cruiser is just three car-lengths behind him. Coming through a downtown intersection with the radio on and the air conditioning on, he may not hear you until you are right at the intersection. Say you are in a pursuit or emergency run and quickly approaching this intersection. He may not hear or see you until all of sudden you are there and both cars collide. As an officer, you owe it to yourself and to the general public to pay attention, drive defensively, and expect that the motorist will not see your emergency lights or hear your siren. Drive accordingly.

Driving is said to be 90 percent mental and 10 percent physical, which places a

heavy emphasis on the need to concentrate. This is especially true of police enforcement driving. The driver must take in a vast amount of information from a constantly changing environment. He must decide if, when, and how much to use the steering wheel, accelerator, and brake.

With speed-sensitive power steering, fuel-injected engines, and ABS-controlled power disc brakes, the job of physically controlling the vehicle is relatively easy. Traction control and antilock brakes have relieved the driver of some of the mental demands. However, the mental tasks of "when and how much" still exist. The loss of vehicle control is almost always due to one of three things: turning the steering wheel too much, applying the brakes too late or too hard, and getting on the gas too soon or too hard. Each of these is a mental decision.

Physically turning the steering wheel is relatively easy. Deciding when and how far to turn the wheel is more difficult.

Think Ahead and Let the Chase Come to You

The 18th District of Chicago's near north side includes such areas as the Rush street nightclub strip, Old Town, the North Clark Street "skid row" section, Cabrini-Green public housing project, and the "Magnificent Mile" of North Michigan Avenue. This area is hardly conducive to the high-speed pursuits featured on so many of the police video shows seen on televisions today. Congestion and near gridlock conditions on weekend evenings are common place.

Chicago Police units that worked this area practiced procedures that were and are quite different from those that are taught in police training academies today. Chases in those parts of the city were generally of short duration. Fleeing vehicles quickly lost the pursuing squad in traffic by turning up side streets, or the drivers abandoned their vehicles and fled on foot because of congestion.

Over time, officers of the district learned to adapt their tactics. For example, they learned to have only one or two units do the actual chasing. Nothing was gained by having a "parade" of flashing, squawking squad cars trailing after a fleeing vehicle. Any nearby units monitoring the chase would begin paralleling the chase on adjoining streets. Many times in the heat of the chase, a fleeing driver turned onto a side street only to find another squad car coming directly at him. Chicago side streets (only one lane with bumper-to-bumper parked cars on both sides of the street) are not conducive to maneuvering past a vehicle coming directly at you, so the chase usually ended right there.

I remember one incident in which I was riding with a relatively new officer. A chase started on Rush Street and was winding up and down streets in the immediate area. The new officer was all hot and bothered, wanting to get in on the chase. I explained to him that it was a Saturday night and the chase was going nowhere. I could hear several units calling out the location of the fleeing vehicle as it turned and squirmed and reversed its course in the highly congested area. I pulled over to the curb in my unmarked vehicle, facing northbound on Dearborn Street and told the rookie that we were going to wait and let the chase come to us.

Within a few minutes, we saw the fleeing car turn off of westbound Elm Street to a very congested southbound Dearborn Street. The car pulled over to the curb, and the two suspects got out and ran to a nearby building where they huddled into a window well in the gangway between two apartment buildings. My amazed partner and I simply walked up and stood over the two suspects and arrested them. They were both wanted in connection with burglary and were being pursued after threatening a pedestrian with a firearm. So much for "high speed" chases in congested areas of large cities.

This scenario isn't uncommon in the city. Knowing the streets, the most likely routes the fleeing vehicle will take, and letting the chase come to you results in successful apprehension of offenders more times than not. Individual officers should also talk over their strategies of pursuit ahead of time so that while in pursuit, an officer can be confident that there are other supporting units around him to pick up the chase when the fleeing vehicle eludes the pursuing squad in a congested area.

—Bill Reynolds
Chicago Police Department (Retired)

Attitude and Judgment

Even if you concentrate on driving, driver attitude also influences the eventual outcome of an emergency run or pursuit. This is because a poor driver attitude contributes to more accidents than does a lack of skill. Attitude affects good judgment on how to drive the car. Attitude is a person's manner of acting, feeling, or thinking that shows his or her disposition. Good judgment is the person's ability to perceive hazards or dangers and respond accordingly to avoid an accident or loss of control.

Be confident, but be sure your confidence is based on training and experience. Don't be overconfident. Allow for mistakes or unpredictable actions on the part of other drivers. Drive with a margin for error, especially during high-speed runs and pursuits.

Don't let your confidence come from experience alone. You may have been driving incorrectly and making mistakes, and the mistakes simply have not yet caught up to you. Get training. Don't rely on day-to-day experiences. Don't be confident in your driving abilities just because you have had years of street experience. You should have in-service training to remind you of the basics and correct your mistakes.

Your confidence will be enhanced by your success in previous emergency response situations. Although confidence is very important, it does not guarantee success. Experience develops bad habits just as easily as good habits. Practice does not make perfect. Only perfect practice makes perfect.

Both psychological and physiological factors affect your attitude and ability to concentrate, which can increase the potential for collision. These include boredom from spending a full day in the vehicle. The aggressive nature of many officers may also carry over into the driving task. Aggressiveness is not always a useful attribute in emergency driving. Often, it results in high-risk behavior. The attitude of some officers is that it is okay to drive fast and hard without due regard for the longevity of the vehicle.

Overconfidence in one's driving ability or in the handling capabilities of a law enforcement vehicle can be a mistake. So can not being prepared for the lack of reaction or overreaction from the motoring public in response to seeing a law enforcement vehicle.

The distraction of traditional law enforcement work can cause collisions. These come from using equipment such as radio, radar, spotlights, mobile terminals, etc. Driving at high speeds itself puts a greater demand on your searching and visual skills. Fatigue associated with long time spans in the vehicle can take its toll on your attitude. This includes fatigue from being on a rotating shift when your biological clock is telling you that it is time to sleep. Your attitude can very much affect your decision-making in emergency responses. If you have an attitude that makes you think that you are above the law because you are a law enforcement officer or that you must get an offender at all costs, you will make bad decisions which could endanger yourself and others.

Emotions are an overwhelming factor in decision-making. You need to try to control your emotions and to keep them in check to the greatest possible extent. You do this through your knowledge, your ongoing evaluation of driving conditions, and your estimates of the possible risks involved.

Stress is inevitable. You cannot eliminate it, but you can try to control it. As a driver, your stress level will increase as you feel you are losing control of your vehicle or the space around your vehicle. Stress is the reverse of control.

4

Braking Techniques: With ABS and Without

Brakes are wonderful—they can get you out of trouble. They can also cause a loss of control and even more trouble. A lot of cars with regular, non-ABS (Antilock Braking System) brakes are still on the road today. If you get into an emergency in a non-ABS car and slam on the brakes, you will lock up the front wheels. When you lock the front tires, you have lost rolling friction.

Rolling friction is traction, and traction is needed for steering. With locked brakes, you have no more steering. You can turn the wheel all the way to the left and all the way to the right, and you will still continue going straight. If you are driving around a curve, you will go in a straight line off the road. If you are driving in a straight line, you will continue to go straight into what you were trying to avoid by putting on your brakes. If you are in that panic braking situation in a non-ABS car, you could pump the brakes. During pumping, the pedal pressure is momentarily released, which allows the brakes to unlock. This allows the tires to roll and gives your steering back. Actually, that is what the Antilock Braking System does, except it locks and unlocks the brakes 10 times a second, which is far faster than even a professional driver can do.

You could also back off the brake pedal pressure to the level called "threshold braking." This is where the brakes are almost locked but not quite. They are still rolling

The most common braking error during a panic stop or an accident avoidance is locking the brakes. *Larry Hollingsworth*

but on the threshold of locking. Actually, this is where we get maximum braking power. However, applying this precise amount of pedal pressure in a true panic situation is tough, even for the best drivers.

ABS was developed to help achieve threshold braking in panic situations and to help correct steering problems caused by locked brakes. ABS does not necessarily stop the car in a shorter distance, but it does allow the car to be steered during near-maximum braking.

When the brakes are totally locked up, they stop the wheels from turning, and all you have between you and the road are four tire patches. When the front wheels are locked up, the result is no steering control.

How ABS Works

ABS is a computerized brake system with sensors on all four brake rotors or drums. The computer automatically detects if any of the tires are locked, or rotating at a slower speed than the others or at a lower speed than the vehicle itself is traveling. Once it senses the locked brake, the ABS pumps the brakes much faster than a human can. It pulsates the brakes on and off rapidly. This allows the front wheels to start to lock up and then release in order to continue to rotate. The result is rolling friction that permits steering.

In terms of safety, ABS is probably the best thing in the history of the automobile. The problem is, most people don't understand ABS and don't use it properly. ABS works independently on all four wheels. If you slam on the brakes, the computer takes over and simply pumps the brakes for you, more quickly than you could yourself. When you put the brakes on hard, you feel the brake pedal pulsating under your foot and you hear it going "duh-duh-duh." That is the ABS at work. If the ABS computer goes out, you can still pump the brakes and make them work.

ABS brakes got off to a bad start with a lot of law enforcement officers when they were first put on police cars in 1991. It was assumed that police officers understood how ABS brakes worked, including the pulsating pedal. While Mercedes, BMW, and other European cars have had ABS for a long time, it was totally new to most cops. They had to be taught that the ABS brakes would not lock, taught not to pump the brakes during emergency stopping, taught that the pedal would pulsate and even kick back a little when activated, and taught that the pedal would be a little lower before maximum braking.

This was a lot to teach every police officer in the United States. Over the next few years, with both Ford and GM active in educating the police on the characteristics and advantages of ABS, cops got up to speed on antilock brakes. ABS had a controversial start but is now a widely understood and accepted safety device.

How do you know whether the ABS is functional, or whether your squad car even has ABS? Not all police package sedans have ABS. Say you are taking a different squad car out today. Even at 10 miles per hour you can tell whether you have ABS or if it is working. Problems with ABS are rare, but possible. At about 10 or 15 miles per hour, step on the brake hard. If you feel the brake

When locked brakes on a non-ABS car fail to slow the car fast enough, some drivers push the brake pedal even harder.
Larry Hollingsworth

Tires must be rolling to allow the car to steer. Locked brakes do not allow the driver to steer. *Larry Hollingsworth*

Accident investigators frequently see four black marks leading right to the obstacle the driver was trying to avoid. *Larry Hollingsworth*

Even in the late 1990s, many police cars do not have ABS. ABS is either an extra cost option or a delete for credit. *Larry Hollingsworth*

The key to braking in a non-ABS vehicle is to pump the brakes or to brake at the threshold of brake lock up. *Larry Hollingsworth*

pedal pulsate under your foot or hear it go "duh-duh-duh," you know you have ABS and that it is working. Checking for a working ABS is a good habit to develop whatever vehicle you drive.

Using ABS

ABS can be used when your car starts to hydroplane—when water on the roadway is deeper than the tread in your tires. The tires actually ride up on the layer of water and lose contact with the road surface. With an ABS-equipped car, when you come off the gas and stand on the brakes, ABS will pulsate the brake system, pumping it on-off-on-off, giving you bits of traction to help you slow. The same thing is true in the snow or on ice. On ice, it is going to feel as if you are never going to make it, but the ABS actually does help to steer the car. The car just reacts more slowly because of the extreme lack of traction.

Do not not pump the brakes on an ABS-equipped car. ABS is activated when one wheel locks or rotates much slower than any other wheel. ABS is deactivated when the pedal pressure is backed off, and all four wheels rotate at the same speed. By pumping the brakes, you turn on and then turn off the ABS, which greatly reduces its effectiveness. Simply let the computer do the job for you. It can provide near-maximum stopping power and let you worry about steering around an obstacle in an emergency.

All you need to remember with ABS brakes is to stand on the brakes as hard as you want and turn the wheel to make a lane change. If you are in a slide, stand on the brakes and steer where you want to go. It's as simple as that. When you are done with the braking, then and only then, get off the brakes. Don't be in the middle of braking with ABS, trying to turn and avoid something, and then ease off the brakes. Then you go back into conventional braking.

A common problem drivers have with ABS is that they forget they have ABS. They slam the brakes on when they have to stop. When the pedal starts to pulsate or modulate, they think something is wrong with the brakes. They either pump the ABS brakes, or they release the brake pedal pressure and it goes back into the normal brake system. If you try to pump the brakes on a car with ABS, the system will not react quickly enough, and you will have a much harder time stopping. When you feel the ABS pedal working, pulsing on and off, under your foot, push down harder. Keep it down until you have completed the maneuver.

ABS has one fantastic feature that most people don't know about. Suppose you're coming around the corner on a slippery road. All of a sudden the back end slides out and you get into an oversteer, or a rear-wheel slide. Get on the brakes and turn into the direction of the skid. The ABS detects which tires have traction and which ones

Maximum braking power comes from tires that are rolling but almost locked. Rolling friction also allows the car to respond to steering inputs. *Larry Hollingsworth*

Whether it is brake and turn, or brake, turn, and stop, the key to vehicle control is not to lock the brakes. *Larry Hollingsworth*

The lesson from the Bondurant Brake and Turn exercise is simple. With the brakes locked, the driver loses steering.

ABS in Action

One day at the Ford Proving Grounds in Naples, Florida, I was doing some hot laps with dealers in a Ford Thunderbird as part of a driving demonstration. We were doing 70-mile per hour four-wheel power slides (four-wheel drifts) through some corners and everybody loved it. Ford's chief engineer for ABS, Bob Eaton, offered to show me how ABS really works. I thought I knew how it worked. I knew you could stop quick with it. I knew you could stop while turning to avoid something. As it turned out, I really didn't know what else it could do.

The Ford engineer taught me ABS will also correct a slide around a corner. With the engineer riding along, we went through a corner at 70 miles per hour. In the middle of a power slide through the corner, he told me to jam on the brakes. I looked to the left and to the right. There were grassy areas on both sides of the road where I figured I would end up when I ran off the road. I figured the rear brakes would lock up and spin me around. I got on the brakes anyhow, steered where I wanted to go, and brought the car under complete control. ABS straightened the car out of my power slide, which had turned into a slide, and brought me to a stop. I couldn't believe it.

On the next set of corners, the engineer told me to go in too fast, put the car into a deliberate understeer situation (front-wheel skid), and about 3 feet before we drive off the road, to stand on the brakes and steer the car where I wanted it to go. ABS brought me right out of the slide and to a stop. I was so impressed that I used the ABS the rest of the day during the hot laps. I now do that as a normal demonstration to Ford dealers, to our students, and to anyone that I have a chance to demonstrate ABS. ABS is fantastic. As far as safety goes, it is the best thing that has come along in the history of the automobile.

Practice the technique. Wet down a large parking lot or other large area and drive in a large circle. As you start to accelerate around the circle, the car will understeer and you will get a front-wheel slide. Then just get on the brakes. You will feel the brakes pulsate. All of a sudden the slide stops and you are tracking around the corner the way you want. Try that several times. Then try it with a rear-wheel slide.

If the rear won't come out, lift off the gas quickly while turning. The weight will transfer forward. Then floor the gas. The back end will slide out. Maintain the slide a little bit and then get on the brakes. You will feel the ABS working. Turn into the skid.

—*Bob Bondurant*

do not. The ABS computer is constantly comparing the rotation speed of each of the four tires to all the others. In this case, the rear tires have less traction than the front. The ABS pulses all the brakes. However, it applies more brakes to the rear and less to the front in an attempt to get all four tires rotating at the same speed again. As a result of different amounts of braking on the front than the rear, the ABS helps to correct the oversteer. You can turn into the slide and come out of it. ABS works to regain control, whether it is a front-wheel slide or a rear-wheel slide. The car will recover as if it were on a dry street.

Non-ABS Braking Techniques

Your squad car may not have ABS. It remains an extra cost option, or a delete-for-credit, even on many late-model police cars. On a non-ABS car, your two best braking options are to pump the brakes as rapidly as you possibly can, or to use threshold braking.

Let's talk about braking without ABS. If you are coming down the center lane and you have to suddenly make a left-lane change and come to a stop, lift off the gas. Weight is going to transfer forward to put more traction on the front. Turn and start braking. Do not slam on the brakes. If you do, you will lock up all four brakes. When this happens, you lose rolling friction and traction. You will slide into what you were trying to avoid.

In a non-ABS car, think of the brake pedal as a big sponge. Squeeze the brakes on firmly and make the lane change. If you find you have suddenly locked up the rear wheels, the rear end of the car is going to get into a slide. If you start in that situation then pump the brake on and off, on and off. Don't pump the brakes too fast. If you pump the brake too fast, the

The driver can turn the wheels all the way left or right, but with locked brakes, the car goes straight.

With locked brakes, the driver should back off the pedal just slightly (threshold braking) or pump the brakes. Most drivers just do nothing.

brakes don't have time to release and begin rolling again. You must have rolling friction to keep the tire patches working for you.

Threshold braking is just short of locking the brakes up. It is the maximum braking with steering control. Threshold braking is the primary braking technique used by race car drivers, however. It requires a lot of practice and extreme concentration. Even some highly skilled race drivers lock up all four tires in a panic stop on the race track.

If you lock up the front wheels when you are trying to turn, the car will go straight. At

In terms of safety, ABS brakes are the biggest advance in the history of the automobile. The ABS computer module automatically pumps the brakes during heavy brake pedal pressure.

The advantage of ABS is NOT shorter stopping distances. A driver using threshold braking can stop in less distance than when using ABS.

One real advantage of ABS brakes is the ability to turn while braking at maximum levels.

Another advantage of ABS brakes is the ability to quickly stop in a panic. Under panic braking, most drivers forget to threshold brake or pump the brakes.

In a car without ABS, or with ABS deactivated, it is easy to lose steering and braking control under wet conditions.

If you entered a curve too fast or suddenly hit a slick spot, it can be difficult to brake and turn in a car without ABS.

Many single car accidents happen because of errors while braking. ABS can help prevent some of these errors.

that point, just relax the calf muscle on the leg used to apply brake pressure. That will be just enough reduction in brake pressure to release the front-wheel lockup or rear wheel lock up.

In a panic stop, your first reaction is to lock up the brakes. When this does not slow you down enough, the normal reaction is to apply even more pressure to lock up the brakes, front or rear, that are not already locked up. The mistaken myth is that locked brakes produce the maximum stopping power. That is not true.

In a panic stop, if you have either the front or the rear wheels locked, you must back off the pedal pressure to brake harder. You want to be almost locked, not actually locked. With threshold braking, you are just on the verge of locking the brakes. Properly done, threshold braking will stop the car in a shorter distance than either ABS or especially pumping the brakes.

However, threshold braking takes a lot of practice. Since most motorists, including police officers, do not practice enough and have a tendency to lock the brakes in a panic stop, ABS was invented. As a side benefit when threshold braking, you still have full directional control. You can turn

while braking, just like with ABS. Remember that tires can not turn if 100 percent of the traction is used for braking. You will have to relax the threshold braking pressure even more as you go from a straight line to turning. Use threshold braking if suddenly your ABS stops working. You can still stop and have steering control.

The best advice for a panic reaction is to practice what you would do before you are in a panic situation. You can do this in your car or in your living room at home. Push down very hard with your right foot and relax your lower calf muscle slightly, release, push down again and release your calf muscle again. Practice this once a day until you get used to it so you can react to that situation.

Practice by taking your car out where there is no traffic. Slam on the brakes at 25 miles per hour and feel the front wheels lock up. Turn the wheels a little to the left, you will find yourself going straight. Brake hard, hear the tires squeal, release your calf muscle, back on again, release your calf muscle, again and again, and you will find you have steering control. You will have to really think and concentrate on how to do this maneuver. If you practice it, you can make that work for you in an emergency situation.

ABS can help pull you out of a slide. If you feel the car losing control, get on the brakes hard enough to activate the ABS.

The Bondurant School has a corner set up in a large flat area for the "Brake-and-Turn exercise." You come down the straightaway at 50 miles per hour. Just as you start into the corner, you slam on the brakes as hard as you can. In a non-ABS car, you will lock the front wheels up and go straight. You can push on the brakes as hard as you want and turn the steering wheel all the way to the left, but you will go absolutely straight ahead. The next time you come down the straight, you slam on the brakes in a panic stop, lock the brakes, then pump the brake pedal. This gets enough traction to the front tires to make the corner. Pumping the brakes during a panic stop takes some training.

Trail Braking Technique

On the topic of braking, remember the trailing brake technique. Trail braking is a term and a technique pioneered by Bob Bondurant himself. The braking technique dates back to his Corvette racing days on the twisting Riverside road racing course in California. Bob found that lap times around this particular race course greatly improved by coming off the brakes slowly and maintaining some braking pressure on some of the sections of the track. This kept the weight on the front tires longer, which gave them needed traction in some of the turns.

Releasing braking pressure as you turn is known as trail braking. As you turn into the corner, start to release the brake pedal pressure very slowly and very gradually. Braking transfers the weight forward, compressing the front springs, giving you a larger front tire patch. This means good traction on the front.

You want to maintain that front tire traction going into the first third of the way around the corner. If it is a 90-degree corner, trail brake halfway around the corner.

ABS is designed to make sure all four wheels are rotating at the same speed. In a slide, understeer, or oversteer, the tires at the ends of the car rotate at different speeds. ABS modulates the brakes at the two ends to regain equal rotational speed. This corrects the slide!

With ABS, keep your foot hard on the brakes and steer where you want the car to go. Don't back off the ABS until the problem is over.

Use less and less brake pedal pressure but keep some pressure on the brakes to keep the front tire patches working for you. When you notice that the front end is sliding out at the corner, ease on more brake pedal pressure. Remember your calf muscle.

As you decelerate from 100 miles per hour to make a 30-mile per hour intersection, use a trailing brake as you go into the corner. Transfer weight forward to the front for maximum tire patch and maintain that traction as you turn into the corner. Then relaxing your calf muscle gradually, slowly letting the brakes come off, keeping the downforce on the front tires and outside tire. By the time you are through the corner, your braking will be done. Squeeze on the throttle slightly to transfer weight to the rear wheels, and then add more throttle.

Brake Fade

During a long pursuit or emergency run when you are pushing your car too hard, your brakes can get so hot they actually boil the brake fluid inside the brake calipers. This causes the brake fluid to go from a liquid to a gas (air). While a liquid is almost impossible to compress, a gas is very easy to compress. Fluid gives the brakes a very solid pedal. Boiled brake fluid with gas bubbles in the lines and in the caliper pistons gives the brakes a very soft pedal. Brake fluid doesn't get to calipers to move the brake piston out to the discs to help the car slow down. Even extreme pedal pressure does not slow the car down. This is brake fade.

One word of caution on ABS brakes. The fastest way to overheat the brakes is to activate the ABS on every stop during a pursuit. When ABS is activated, the brakes are greatly heated. The best way to use ABS is to not engage it. Save it for a panic situation. Especially during extended pursuit driving, be careful to stay out of ABS mode. You can brake very hard without activating ABS and without overheating your brakes. The police package cars have large enough brakes to allow an almost indefinite use of brakes this way, provided short stretches of road are available to allow the brakes to cool. However, a continual use of ABS will overheat the brakes and cause enough brake fade to result in a loss of control. Concentrate, be aware, and pay attention to avoid brake fade.

5
Skid Control/
Skid Avoidance

A front-wheel slide is called "understeer," sometimes called "push" by race drivers. Understeer is where the front tires lose traction regardless of the tire patch size. If the front tires lose traction, the driver loses steering. As a result, the car turns less into the corner than the driver wants. It "under" steers. The car will continue in a more or less straight line instead of turning. This means the car will run off the road during a left-hand turn or turn so wide in a right-hand turn that the car goes into the oncoming traffic lane and then off the road.

The opposite of this is a rear-wheel slide, called "oversteer." In this case, the rear wheels lose traction and the rear end swings to the outside of the corner. This causes the front end to point "more" into the corner than the driver wants. It "over" steers. The car will either run off the road to the inside of the turn on a right-hand corner or run into the oncoming traffic lane on a left-hand corner. In either case, the back end of the car may come completely around and the car will spin totally out of control.

Understeer occurs when the front tires lose traction, and as a result, lose some steering control. The car turns "less" into the corner than the driver wants. It "under" steers. *Rick Scuteri*

Avoiding Understeer

Understeer is caused by one of three conditions. These are (1) carrying too much speed into a corner, (2) getting on the throttle too soon on corner exit, and (3) braking hard enough to lock up the front tires.

Too much speed is easy to understand. The limits of adhesion are simply exceeded. To fix this kind of understeer, simply take your foot off the accelerator and brake smoothly, or if you're already on the brakes, apply more braking pressure. Both actions transfer weight forward to the front wheels, which increases the tire patch size and tire traction. This also, of course, slows the car down, correcting the original problem.

Too much throttle or getting on the throttle too soon transfers weight off the front tires. Even though the tires are turned in at exactly the same angle, the car does not respond to this angle. It underresponds or understeers because the weight is off the front tires reducing the front tire patch and traction. To fix this kind of understeer, simply ease off the gas to transfer weight forward onto the front tires, increasing the tire patch sizes and traction.

Braking hard enough to lock the tires causes understeer, or rather "no-steer." Remember, if the brakes are locked, you cannot steer the car. You can turn the steering wheel left or right but the direction of the car will not change at all. A tire must rotate in order to have traction and must have traction in order to steer the car. To fix this kind of understeer, relax the brake pedal pressure. This allows the wheels to rotate again and steering control will return immediately. This is the lesson from the Brake and Turn Exercise.

Relaxing brake pressure is NOT the normal reaction. In fact, the normal reaction is to apply the brakes harder. When this happens, the car will continue head-long and crash into the obstacle you were trying to avoid or run straight off the road in the middle of a turn. Veteran traffic officers have seen evidence of this time and again: four black rubber marks leading straight to the impact. Had the driver lifted off the

Oversteer occurs when the rear tires lose traction, and the rear of the car swings to the outside of the corner. This causes the front end to point "more" in the corner than the driver wants. It "over" steers. *Rick Scuteri*

Understeer is caused by too much speed into the corner, on the throttle too soon during corner exit, and by braking hard enough to lock up the front tires.

This Mustang GT mounted on the SkidCar platform shows severe understeer. The front wheels are turned sharply but the car is not responding. This could be due to too much throttle, which takes weight off the front tires. Ease off the throttle. *Rick Scuteri*

This Taurus SHO mounted on a SkidCar platform is going straight, even though the wheels are turned to the left. That is a front-wheel slide called understeer. The solution on a front-wheel drive car is to cadence brake. If that does not work, then cadence throttle.

brake pedal at any time during the problem and turned the steering wheel, the collision would have probably been avoided.

Avoiding Oversteer

Oversteer is caused by one of three conditions. These are (1) braking too aggressively entering into a corner, (2) too much acceleration out of a corner and (3) aggressive braking that locks the rear brakes.

The solution to this kind of oversteer is to take your foot off the brake to allow some weight to transfer back to the rear wheels. This is not a natural reaction to oversteer, but is the correct reaction to control the rear end. Then turn into the slide as the car stabilizes and straighten the wheel out again as the car recovers from the slide.

Too much acceleration out of a corner can actually cause the rear wheels to spin. This has exactly the same affect on traction as the tires being locked. Spinning rear tires causes the rear end to lose traction. As you accelerate, weight transfers to the rear, increasing tire patch size. However, the rear tires can only handle so much side force regardless of the tire patch or amount of weight transfer. A spinning tire and a locked brake have the same lack of traction. A spinning or locked wheel have the same lack of traction.

To fix this kind of oversteer, simply back off the gas to reduce wheel spin. Of course, you should still turn into the direction of the spin for a steering correction.

Aggressive braking that locks the rear wheels causes oversteer from loss of traction just as when the rear wheels are spinning. The back of the car is very susceptible to very small steering wheel inputs. A slight turn of the steering wheel with locked (or spinning) rear tires will cause the rear end to spin around quickly.

Locking up the rear brakes anywhere in a turn, including entering the turn, will have the same affect. The fix for this kind of oversteer is to get off the brakes just enough to get the rear wheels turning again. The rotating tires will restore traction, yet the brake pressure can still be applied. This, of course, is the secret behind the 180 degree turns: lock the rear tires with the emergency brake, turn the steering wheel to get the back end to spin around, then release the parking brake to get traction to the rear wheels.

A natural progression from understeer may be oversteer. Oversteer means simply that the vehicle points itself in a direction that will tighten up its turning radius. The rear tires exceed the limit of cohesion, and the back end of the car skids toward the outside of the turn. Oversteer can be the result of sudden, rough steering movements, sudden application or withdrawal of the throttle, reduced adhesion due to water, or a progression of understeer.

When a vehicle is understeering in a turn because of excessive speed or throttle

Oversteer is caused by too much acceleration out of a corner, braking too aggressively coming into a corner, or hard braking that locks the rear tires. With an oversteering car, instantly correct for the slide with the steering wheel by turning it in the direction you want to go. *Rick Scuteri*

application, tremendous stress is placed on the front tires, wheels, and suspension. The front tires sliding sideways have the same effect of braking with the front wheels. As this stress reduces the vehicle's speed, traction will be regained by the front tires, which are now turned sharper than necessary to negotiate the radius of the turn. At this point, the vehicle turns abruptly toward the inside of the curve, which causes the rear tires to exceed cohesion, and the car almost instantly attains a condition of oversteer. The problem here is that the driver's attempt to correct the slide will be almost always too late or too slow. The oversteer will become a spinout with complete loss of control.

If the oversteer is a result of excessive throttle or rough steering while in a curve, control would normally be regained by smoothly letting up on the throttle and simultaneously turning the front wheels toward the outside of the curve. The oversteer could be maintained by reapplying enough throttle to again spin the rear wheels, then reducing throttle while steering. Excessive throttle applied to an oversteering vehicle can result in a spinout regardless of efforts to steer out of it.

Skid Control with The Bondurant SkidCar

One of the most important exercises at The Bondurant School is skid control. Students drive a specially designed SkidCar. The instructor can separately control the front end traction and the back end traction of the SkidCar to produce any degree of understeer or oversteer. With an electronic controller, the instructor uses hydraulics to raise and lower the training vehicle in 10 different and adjustable increments. This increases or decreases the contact patch and traction between the tires and the road. The instructor can duplicate literally any road condition including dry pavement, wet pavement, gravel roads, muddy roads, slushy snow, loose or packed snow, and even glare ice.

The front and rear wheels are controlled separately. This allows the instructor to dial in any amount of understeer (front-wheel loss of traction) or oversteer (rear-wheel loss of traction) or one then the other. The instructor can vary the amount of traction silently, in any amount, and while the vehicle is being driven.

The SkidCar is an interactive training device. The issue is not speed but vehicle dynamics. The SkidCar takes speed out of the equation, as everything happens at very low speeds. The driver can first see the skid start and then feel it happen. He or she has enough reaction time to learn about stopping skids before they escalate and to react to the dynamics of the skid as it happens. The driver has time to control the vehicle by steering inputs and weight transfer, and the instructors have time during the early phases of the skid to actually coach the driver. The SkidCar duplicates the vehicle dynamics, but only simulates the vehicle speed.

According to the Virginia Division of Training and Standards, the most common driver errors are too much throttle, too much braking, steering too much, being too rough or aggressive with the vehicle, and the improper use of the eyes while driving. An estimated 85 percent of loss-of-control accidents are from over use of the steering and brakes. Most drivers fail to look in the right direction during a skid or far enough ahead while driving.

The SkidCar gives immediate feedback to all of these faults. It will spin like a top if driven wrong or instantly recover from a near-guardrail experience if the driver simply shifts his eyes to where he wants the car to go. The big difference between the SkidCar and other driver training is that with the SkidCar, the driver induces the skid, not the instructor. The driver can choose to avoid the skid by correct vehicle control, rather than being forced to react to a skid caused by the instructor. The vehicle puts the responsibility for vehicle control where it belongs, with the driver.

The severity or degree to which oversteer has progressed will determine whether or not a driver can regain control. If oversteer has progressed beyond the suspension geometry of the vehicle's steering, the car will continue to pivot around the front wheels and spin out. The front wheels of most cars will turn approximately 20 degrees from straight ahead to steering lock. Thus, if the rear of the car is allowed to skid beyond 20 degrees before the driver starts to correct his steering, efforts at regaining control will be futile. For this reason, the officer must react immediately and almost instinctively during a skid. The higher the speed, the faster the driver must react to regain control.

A "four-wheel drift" occurs when a cornering vehicle is above the limits of adhesion AND in a balanced understeer versus oversteer condition. The car is pointed in the direction it is traveling and all wheels are following a line of the curve, however, the car is evenly drifting or skidding toward the outside of the curve. If there is adequate roadway available, the vehicle may make it around the turn successfully.

The danger of the four-wheel drift is the absence of any margin of safety. Any sudden change of steering, throttle, or brakes will upset the delicate balance of the vehicle and result in loss of control. An officer suddenly faced with any traffic hazard would be virtually helpless to avoid a collision. A true four-wheel drift can be attained and utilized in the controlled environment of a race track, but should not be deliberately attempted on public roads in a police car.

Aggressive braking while cornering causes too much weight to shift too rapidly from the rear to the front. The rear tire patches suddenly get too small while the front tires have plenty of downforce and traction. This is no problem as long as the car is braking in a straight line. In a corner, however, a lot less traction on the rear compared to the front causes the rear end to slide to the outside. This is the "throttle-off" oversteer. When an officer suddenly lifts off the gas and suddenly stabs the brakes, and weight is transferred from the rear wheels to the front wheels, leaving the rear tire patches too small to maintain control of the rear end.

When you abuse the throttle by lifting off the throttle abruptly, you actually affect the steering. The back end is going to want to swing around and put you into a slide or spin. Roll off the gas smoothly to avoid sudden weight transfer. If the back end does start to slide out when you have jumped off the throttle too quickly, get back on the throttle slightly to transfer weight back on the rear tires. Most of all, be smooth with the throttle. That is all it takes to prevent throttle-off oversteer.

Throttle Steering

We can actually steer the car with the throttle instead of the steering wheel. Use both the throttle and the brake as a way to steer when you drive a car. When you come into a corner, you roll off the gas. As you turn the wheel, you gently squeeze on the brakes which transfers the weight forward and sets the chassis by compressing front springs. Then you squeeze on the gas to steer the car through the corner.

Weight transfer occurs during braking and accelerating. When a vehicle is accelerated, weight is transferred to the rear. This can increase traction and help a driver retain or regain control. An example could be a moderate oversteer in which a smoothly applied throttle might help gain enough traction with the rear wheels to straighten out the vehicle's course. Applying the brakes transfers weight to the front end.

If too much forward weight transfer is gained at curve entry, the lightened rear end may be induced to oversteer. Forward weight transfer can also have an adverse effect prior to traversing dips, chuck-holes, railroad crossings, or the like. Hard braking at this point compresses the front suspension, and lowers vehicle height, when clearance and suspension movement is most critically needed. A driver unexpectedly encountering these hazards should brake and reduce speed as much as possible, then release the brakes as the vehicle crosses the hazard.

The Bondurant Throttle Steer Circle proves that the car can be steered with the gas pedal alone. In normal situations, the experienced driver uses the gas and the brake in addition to the steering wheel to steer the car.

With the steering wheel held in a fixed position, the officer accelerates smoothly. This transfers weight off of the front tires and on to the rear tires.

The Throttle Steer Circle

One of the first maneuvers students practice at The Bondurant School is the Throttle Steer Circle. As the name implies, we use the throttle to steer the car. The course has a 125-foot diameter inner circle and a 375-foot diameter outer circle. The officer runs with his inside front tire about 6 feet off the inside circle at about 15 miles per hour. The steering wheel is turned to whatever angle is needed to hold 15 miles per hour around the inner circle. With the steering wheel set in that exact position, the officer slowly presses the accelerator.

This exercise demonstrates that a car can be steered with only the throttle. Each officer puts his vehicle in a constant radius turn, cornering at a speed close to the adhesion limit of the car. Without moving the steering wheel but by simply adding more gas, the nose of the car moved out to form a larger diameter circle. More throttle took weight off the front tires and reduced the contact patches thus reducing traction. Without moving the wheel but by simply letting off the gas, the squad car turned sharply to the center of the circle. Letting off the gas transferred weight and downforce to the front tires. They turned the car sharply toward the center of the Throttle Steer Circle.

The officers learn the car can be steered under full control with only the gas pedal and without moving the steering wheel. This is especially important to know when the wheel is already turned to full lock and you need to turn even tighter. Both the throttle and the steering control the direction of the car, using front to rear weight transfer.

As the officer accelerates, weight transfers both from the front to the rear and from the inside tires to the outside tires. This improves traction at the outside and rear tires and reduces traction at the inside and front tires. When the officer accelerates while turning, the springs on the inside front tire release their downforce. The front springs unload and the front tire patch becomes about half the size that it was. The result is less traction on the front. That means, with no movement of the steering wheel, the car will move from the inner circle to the outer circle.

During the throttle steer drill, the officer accelerates until the car reaches the outside white line of the 375-foot circle. When the throttle is backed off, weight will transfer forward again, giving the front tires more traction. Still at the same steering angle as the start of the drill, but now with traction again, the front tires will now pull the car rapidly back into the inner side of the circle. With the steering wheel at the same position, acceleration will move the car to the outside of the turn, while deceleration will move the car to the inside of the turn.

With less weight, smaller tire patches, and less traction on the front tires, the police car pushes to the outside of the circle. The steering wheel has not moved.

The police car has moved from the inner circle to the outer circle simply due to weight transfer. As the officer lifts off the gas, the weight will shift back to the front and the car will turn hard into the inner circle again.

The rear end on this Taurus SHO SkidCar is coming around the corner faster than the front end. That is a rear-wheel slide called oversteer. In most cases, oversteer can be corrected by getting off the gas.

Understeer and oversteer occur in varying degrees of severity. When the steering wheel is turned, the sidewall of the tire is deformed. Although the wheel is turned a certain amount from straight ahead, the tire tread is turned to a lesser degree from straight ahead. The difference in the angle the wheel is turned and the angle of the tread is called the "slip angle." This slip angle, or understeer, is always present when a vehicle is cornering. At low speeds or in moderate curves, it goes unnoticed. However, as speed and cornering forces are increased, the slip angle increases up to the point of sliding. When the traction has been exceeded, an officer may experience the extreme example of understeer, with the front wheels turned completely to lock and the car proceeding straight ahead.

The California Highway Patrol conducted a test to show this slip angle and resulting understeer. At idle speed, a U-turn with the steering locked could be executed in 44 feet, 6 inches. The same turn attempted at 10 miles per hour took 53 feet. When the car was accelerated, short of wheel spin or front tire sliding, the U-turn took 57 feet, 6 inches. Significantly, at idle speed the U-turn was completed in 6.5 seconds. At the higher rate of speed, the U-turn not only required an additional 13 feet of roadway, but the elapsed time also increased to 8.7 seconds. This exercise confirms the lessons from the Bondurant Throttle Steer Circle.

Since the throttle can steer the car, now you know why it is so important to always be smooth with the throttle.

Front-wheel, Rear-wheel and Four-wheel Drive

Differences exist between front-wheel drive and rear-wheel drive cars during hard driving and during skid control. Say you are going into a corner a little bit too fast in a front-wheel drive car. You get into a front-wheel slide called understeer. This is very common for all cars but especially front-wheel drive cars. The front end is losing traction. If you brake hard with an ABS car, the ABS will detect differences between the front tire lack of traction and the rear tire traction and will correct the slide. If you have a car that does not have ABS, and you're in a front-wheel slide, then you need to cadence brake. Cadence braking is the act of pumping the brake on and off until you start getting little bites of traction, and you find yourself coming out of the skid. front-wheel drive cars do indeed go where the front wheels are pointed.

You may have heard the worst thing that can ever happen in a front-wheel skid in a front-wheel drive car is jump on the gas. You are going to add more skid and have less traction. Say you are on a normal city street and going around a corner a little too fast. You get into front-wheel slide. If you don't execute it right, you are going to be coming head-on into other traffic. First, get off the gas. If the tires don't scrub off enough speed, then go into a cadence throttle: on and off, on and off. That will give you traction.

If you are in a car with rear-wheel drive, and have the same situation, coming around the corner too fast, and all of a sudden the back end is sliding into the on-coming lane of traffic. Turn into the skid and ease the throttle back halfway allowing the tires to scrub the speed off for you. Again, if you have a car with ABS brakes, do the prescribed procedure and then get on the brakes and steer the car where you want it to go.

Now if you have a four-wheel drive vehicle, you have much better traction. You get into a corner and you went a little too fast. You still get into a front-wheel slide or a rear-wheel slide. Ease the throttle off halfway. Let the tires scrub the speed off for you.

Say you have an older four-wheel drive vehicle that does not have ABS. You go through the same corner and get into a front-wheel slide. Pump the throttle (cadence throttle). If that does not work, pump the brakes (cadence brake). Again in either a front- or a rear-wheel slide, don't yank the steering wheel. Instead, turn it in quickly and smoothly, but not too much. In a front-wheel drive vehicle, if you turn into the skid and all of a sudden you want to get back in your lane, the temptation is to yank the wheel back. Just steer it back gently, and in most cases the car will work great. The new Ford police package cars have some form of electronic traction control or traction assist. That gives you more traction. If you start to get into a rear-wheel slide and you accelerate, the electronic traction control takes over. The electronic traction control takes the throttle away from you in small amounts. In a rear-wheel slide, it will help you get out of it. It will smoothly back off the throttle a little bit. Steer in the direction the slide is going, and you will stabilize the car. Electronic traction control is very good. If you stand on the gas too hard, it simply cuts off a couple of cylinders. It keeps the rear wheels from sliding, so you always have traction.

6
Emergency Evasive Maneuvers

According to the National Safety Council (NSC), vehicle accidents are the fourth leading cause of death, behind only heart disease, cancer, and stroke. According to the NSC, passenger cars are involved in 4.1 accidents per million miles. Police cars, in general, are involved in 12.8 accidents per million miles, three times the rate of the motoring public. This accident rate varies by the type of police duty.

The state police and highway patrol are involved in 4.8 accidents per million miles. This is very close to that of the population at large, even though the state police typically drive at very high speeds. The rate for city police and urban county sheriffs' departments is 23.6 accidents per million miles. This is almost six times the general public. Police officers, more than nearly anyone else, need accident avoidance training.

Bob Bondurant developed the most widely copied driver training exercise in the world: the three-lane, traffic-light-controlled "Accident Simulator." At 80 feet away, two of the three green lights turn red and the driver must turn into the light lane.

The accident avoidance drill involves quickly finding the open lane and then lifting off the gas. DO NOT BRAKE.

Lifting off the gas transfers weight onto the front tires, where traction is needed for steering. Only turn the wheel a half-turn.

The lack of knowledge and experience on the part of most drivers causes accidents every single day. They overreact with the wheel, the brakes, and the gas. If drivers—and that includes police officers—knew how to do emergency evasive maneuvers, thousands of lives would be saved.

Let's say one is going down the road, not concentrating and not looking far enough ahead. All of a sudden, a car pulls out in front of me. You jump on the brakes, yank the wheel to miss the car, and without ABS, lock up the front brakes and plow right into the back end of it.

Or say one is in a car with ABS brakes and not paying attention. That person will just slam on the brakes. If one is using the wrong hand position, he or she will yank the wheel too far. The same is also true if one puts the car into a slide and doesn't know what to do with the slide. He or she might turn the steering wheel back the other way and the car spins out.

The way to avoid an accident, using the emergency evasive maneuver, is simple. Lift off the gas—this will transfer weight forward allowing better turning control. Don't touch the brakes. Make a decisive turn to the right or left. If you have been looking ahead and looking back via the mirrors, you know where traffic is around you and you will know which way is open.

Lift off the gas and turn into the open lane. As you're turning into the lane, not more than half a turn, gently squeeze on the throttle. This transfers weight on the rear wheels where it is needed to keep the rear end from spinning around. This is much quicker, and more effective, than trying to brake. If you lift off the gas, turn the wheel and squeeze on the throttle but the once-open lane is now blocked, then you have to brake. With the weight back on the rear end to stabilize it, now apply the brakes hard and come to a stop. Accidents can be avoided if you concentrate, look ahead, and pay attention to traffic. Most of all, don't overreact. Say you are on duty, driving around and just not concentrating. You have one hand on the steering wheel and the other holding a cup of coffee. Suddenly traffic stops in front of you. What will most people do? They lift off the gas quickly, jam the brakes on hard, and yank the wheel to steer away from the car ahead of them. And if you've got one hand with a coffee cup in it, you can't be precise in the way you are steering your car in an emergency. When steering with one hand, most drivers yank the wheel way too far.

Accident Simulator Exercise

At The Bondurant School, we developed the most widely copied driving exercise in the world. This is the three-lane, stoplight-controlled, "Accident Simulator." With incoming speeds of 35 miles per hour, an officer faces three green lights, each controlling a separate traffic lane. When the vehicle is 80 feet away, the lights change.

Once in the open lane, get back on the GAS. This puts weight on the rear tires, where traction is needed to prevent oversteer.

We use the accident simulator for teaching emergency evasive maneuvers. We have three traffic lights set up horizontally. All the lanes are green. You can do the same kind of drill with an instructor sitting next to you. At the right time, they call out which lane is open. You lift off the gas, evaluate which lane is still green. We change the lights on two lanes red. One red light simulates a car stopped in front of you. The other red light simulates a car in that lane so you can't turn into that lane.

As soon as you are beyond the obstacle, you can either brake or turn back to the original lane. Don't brake until the car is straight.

Lift off the gas. Turn into the green lane or the open lane. Use a maximum of a half a turn of the steering wheel. The more you turn the wheel, the tighter the Ackerman steering turns for you. If you turn a full turn, you have turned too much and then you put yourself in a slide. You will come back in a second slide, and all of sudden you will have just spun out.

The proper procedure is to lift off the gas and crank in a half-turn of the wheel to get into the other lane. Midway into the lane, squeeze back on the gas smoothly, not full throttle, to transfer weight to the rear tires, and you are out of the situation much quicker than you might imagine.

This technique is much quicker than if you tried to brake, because when you brake, you slow your maneuvering speed down. In fact, in some situations, you cannot possibly stop in time to avoid a collision. Instead, you must turn to avoid the obstacle. In our simulation, we lift off the gas, turn the wheel, squeeze on the gas, and turn back into the single lane again.

Midway through the lane change, gently squeeze on the gas, transfer the weight to the rear tires, again, compressing the springs and getting a rear tire patch much larger than the front. You now have good rear tire traction. Accelerate smoothly, not abruptly.

The lift, turn, and gas method of accident avoidance gets you by the obstacle quicker than if you try to brake. Some obstacles simply cannot be avoided by braking.

After you have learned the technique, try it with an object in your right hand. You can use anything that simulates a radio microphone head, cell phone, or cup of coffee. As soon as you see the need for a lane change, drop the object quickly. Put your right hand back to the 3 o'clock position. This will restore the 3 and 9 position, because your left hand was already at the 9 o'clock position.

Using both hands on the wheel gives you the most stability and most control. Turn into the open lane with a half-turn of the wheel. If you lift off the gas and turn the wheel, but yank the wheel too far, you're going to spin out. Get back on the gas and turn the wheel back. The car is going to get into a slight rear-wheel skid, so steer slightly into that skid. You are on the gas getting traction to the rear-wheels and back in your own lane.

Another way to do that in a car equipped with ABS brakes is lift, turn, and brake. Remember the ABS pulsates the brake system for you and does not allow the tires to lock up, lose traction, and lose control. So with an ABS car you just lift, turn, and brake in that lane.

If you are driving a car that does not have ABS, it is possible to lock up the front wheels, lose steering, and plow straight ahead. Instead, lift off the gas, turn the wheel, and squeeze on the gas. If you have to brake, the way out of trouble is to simply cadence brake. Pump the brake on and off to get your steering back. Try to drive around the situation that way. Repeat this drill at least a dozen times each way. If you have a car that has ABS, you can practice this drill by pulling the ABS fuse out to disable it.

At The Bondurant School, officers are first given two red lights and a green one. The proper method is to back off the gas and quickly turn the wheel to put the squad car in the lane with the green light. This could be left, center, or right. Just lifting off the gas transferred weight to the front tires, allowing them to turn hard without slipping. This solved only half the problem.

Once the squad car gets in the correct lane after a quick turn, it has a tendency to get very light at the rear end. In order to prevent a rear end spinout at this point, the driver has to apply gas to transfer weight back to the rear tires. The technique is lift, turn, and squeeze. Lift off the gas. Turn the wheel. Squeeze back on the gas smoothly.

A variation on this theme is when all three green lights turn red. The officer has to stop as quickly as possible. You quickly learn that a car with locked brakes takes longer to stop than a car just at the edge of locking. Cadence braking, threshold braking, and ABS braking are the solution, to maximum stopping power and the shortest stopping.

One of the exercises in the "Accident Avoidance Simulator" area gives officers two red lights and one yellow light. On this signal, officers pull into the yellow lane and then emergency stop. This puts both braking and turning forces on the front tires. This almost always locks the front brakes, which gives drivers the opportunity to practice releasing locked-up front brakes. The cars will not turn with locked tires, therefore a cadence pump or a threshold feel is required to get the car stopped in the right lane.

At the end of the exercises, the officers should make a few more passes, not knowing the outcome. This time they should get a green light in an unknown lane, a yellow light in an unknown lane, or all reds. All the aspects of braking and weight transfer come together in this exercise.

7

Low and High Speed Cornering

A good definition of enforcement driving might be an officer's ability to fully use the performance abilities of the vehicle under all driving conditions and in all traffic situations. Very little skill is needed to simply floor the throttle and drive in a straight line. Performance driving involves what to do when it comes time to turn the steering wheel. The three basic considerations when cornering a vehicle are weight, cornering basics, and proper approach.

Weight Transfer and Cornering

All the time you are driving, you must deal with weight transfer. When the car sits statically, all four tire patches are about the same width, about the size of a man's hand. That is all you have between you and the road: four tire patches.

As you accelerate, the car's weight is going to transfer to the rear, compressing the rear springs, giving you downforce on the rear tire patch, thereby increasing the rear

The Bondurant straight-line slalom teaches side-to-side weight transfer. This is done at speeds up to 40 miles per hour with 50-foot cone spacing.

Correctly negotiating the straight-line slalom will create a series of "chirp, chirp, chirp" sounds as the wheel is quickly turned in, then smoothly turned out.

Quickly turn the wheel a half-turn. This suddenly transfers weight to the outside front tire and "plants" it.

tire patch, and it gets larger. The front tire patches in the meantime are getting smaller. As long as you are going in a straight line it doesn't make much difference. If you are accelerating through a corner, however, it can make a big difference.

So as you accelerate through the corner, weight is going to transfer to the rear and to the outside tires giving more traction. The inside tire is going to track through the apex of the corner and have less tire patch. As long as you smoothly accelerate, it won't be a problem. If you stomp on the gas hard, you are going to cause the car to understeer. You only have 11 feet in your driving lane to work with.

If you get into an understeer condition—a front-wheel skid—then slowly and gently ease the throttle back and force the weight to transfer forward on the front tires. The tires cut the speed off. If it is not quite enough, then gently squeeze on the brakes, giving more traction on the front. Steer the car where you want it to be.

Cornering Basics

All corners can be divided into three parts: the entry, the apex, and the exit. An apex is where the car comes closest to the inside edge of the curve. As a rule, the officer should use a late apex cornering technique. This means entering the corner on the outside, getting as much braking done as early as possible, and as much braking in a straight line as possible. Police officers should do 90 percent of their braking in a straight line before turning the steering wheel at all.

An increasing radius corner opens up in diameter, or becomes less sharp, as you drive through the turn. A decreasing radius corner gets tighter and smaller in diameter as you drive through it. A constant radius corner has the same constant and steady diameter. A decreasing radius corner requires more and more brakes as you drive through the turn. An increasing radius corner allows more and more gas to be applied. A constant rate corner requires a steady trail-off of the brakes until the center of the turn, then progressive application of the gas.

Road racing drivers have increasing radius, decreasing radius, and constant radius corners. Each kind of corner calls for a different "line," a different cornering technique with very different braking, turn-in, apex, turn-out, and acceleration points.

The vast majority of enforcement driving involves a 90-degree intersecting road that is best served by the late apex method. The officer only has to remember one method, practice one method, and, most importantly, perform one method under stress.

Plant the wheel, then turn it straight. The drill teaches concentration, steering wheel feel, and throttle control.

Once you reach the next pylon, turn the wheel quickly to plant the outside tire. Stay as close to the pylon as you can.

Race car drivers think about the "apex" and the "line" around a road racing course all the time. In contrast, police officers NEVER think about this. Instead of increasing, decreasing, or constant radius turns, one corner is like every other corner to most cops. As a result, a police officer needs to know how to come into a corner, any corner, slowly enough to stay in his own traffic lane upon exit.

The Approach

The approach should be slow enough to negotiate the corner regardless if it is an early apex (increasing radius), late apex

Side-to-Side Weight Transfer

At The Bondurant School, we teach side-to-side weight transfer with a straight-line slalom. We start out at 25 miles per hour, then 30 miles per hour, then 35 miles per hour, and up to 40 miles per hour driving between cones that are in a straight line and 50 feet apart. As you enter the straight-line slalom, you accelerate to 25 miles per hour and hold that speed all the way through. As you reach the front cone, you give the steering wheel a quick turn. That loads the outside shock and spring and gives the outside tire instant down force. This gives you instant traction on that outside front wheel. These are quick yet smooth inputs, not jerking the wheel.

The key here is to quickly turn the wheel to transfer weight to one side, then smoothly turn the wheel back. When properly done at 40 miles per hour, you'll hear a series of "chirp, chirp,

chirp" sounds as the tires side-load going around the pylons. Without the weight transfer from the rapid side load, you will understeer and won't make it through the slalom without braking.

If you turn the wheel smoothly, the car will start picking up g-forces in the rear end. Pretty soon the rear suspension picks up so much side force that you will spin out. People try to go too fast too soon and that also results in a spin out. The method is to plant the wheel, bring it out straight, plant the wheel, and bring it out straight. As you are planting the wheel, of course, you are turning the direction to the outside of that pylon. In time, you will be able to do this quickly and quite precisely. It teaches you throttle control, steering wheel control, and smoothness, even though you are steering quickly.

—Bob Bondurant

(decreasing radius), or mid apex (constant radius) corner. In fact, the rule is to conservatively treat all corners as late apex corners unless the officer knows different from experience. A late apex requires a steady application of brakes then gas.

The officer should hold to the outside of his lane or the available roadway as long as possible. He will then turn to the inside of

Quickly turn to the left, smoothly straighten it out, then quickly turn the wheel to the right.

The quick-in, smooth-out method keeps the rear suspension from accumulating so much side force that it eventually causes oversteer.

the roadway and touch the inside of the curve, the apex, well after the center of the corner. With all or most of the braking done early, the driver will be able to accelerate past the apex. The officer will be able to see down the straightaway before accelerating. This gives him the most latitude in where to place his car during the exit. To avoid an obstacle, he can steer either to the outside or to the inside of the corner.

The driver turning into the center of the turn (apex) too early will be forced to the outside of the turn on the exit. In the event of an obstacle, or vehicle in the roadway, the only choices for the early apex driver are to collide with the obstacle or run off the road to the outside of the turn.

The two most common driver errors in a high-speed situation are: (1) waiting too long to brake, which carries too much speed into the turn; and (2) turning too soon into the apex, which is the inside part of corner.

For police officers, the entire roadway is limited to just their entire driving lane. The police officer does not have shoulder to shoulder with grassy runoff areas or forgiving tire walls as road racers have. The police officer does not have much room to pull to the inside or drive to the outside. Nor does he have any margin for error. The "runoff area" is lined with telephone poles, cement walls, bridge abutments, and oncoming traffic.

Unlike road racing, in which the driver has great freedom to pick the line through a corner, the line for the officer has already been selected: the narrow driving lane he is in.

Late Apex

One cornering technique that best suits law enforcement driving is the "late apex." The officer brakes early, gets 90 percent of his braking down while in a straight line, stays to the outside of his lane (or the available roadway), until two-thirds of the way through the corner, and comes out under increasing throttle.

The late apex method calls for early braking but also allows early acceleration. In fact, the late apex method allows the officer to accelerate through the apex and apply full acceleration as soon as the wheel is straight.

This also happens to be the most conservative and safest method. The fleeing driver will most likely turn in too soon and wait too long to brake, and will eventually drive off the road. Turning into the corner later and braking earlier will assure that the police officer remains on the roadway. The late apex-early braking method should be used for emergency response driving and pursuit driving alike. It should be used regardless of what line or method the fleeing driver uses.

With a late apex, all the braking is done early, before the officer is committed to a line through the corner. He can even change lanes as he is exiting the corner. He doesn't start to cut into the apex until he can see completely through the turn.

You should reach the closest point to the inside edge of the corner about two-thirds of the way around the corner. Most drivers reach the inside edge of the corner way too soon. Some of them reach the inside of the roadway before the corner even starts, especially on a 90-degree intersection. Reaching the inside edge as you begin to brake and enter the corner is taking an early apex. This is a common and serious mistake.

With an early apex, the braking is done late. The fleeing driver is absolutely committed to one and only one line through the corner. The fleeing driver has no flexibility in the corner exit. A stalled or slower vehicle in his lane will result in a collision or running off the road to avoid a collision. The driver is already using all of his cornering power. He cannot pull tighter to the inside of the roadway. The only option to a collision with a vehicle or pedestrian is to run off the road to the outside.

All curves and corners should be entered at a speed slow enough for the officer to place his car anywhere he chooses as he exits the curve. At high speeds, the car will push to the outside. This method involves early braking, a "late apex," and getting on the throttle as early as possible. The driver hangs to the outside or high side of the curve and gets most of the braking done before entering the curve. This is the race technique for entering a long straight, but police officers should use it for all turns. Applying power while exiting the turn is a much more controllable method than applying brakes while entering the turn.

Police officers should always use the late apex cornering method. Get 90 percent of the braking done early while the car is in a straight line.

With the late-apex method, hold to the outside of the driving lane as long as possible. Begin the turn into the corner late. Trail brake up to the apex.

A turn should always be entered at a speed that is less than maximum. The fact that an officer manages to make it through a corner without spinning out of control does not mean the speed was less than maximum. Less than maximum means the officer can position the patrol car anywhere on the roadway while negotiating the curve.

At maximum speed, the vehicle will understeer and push wide as it goes through the turn. An officer will not be able to change positions in his own lane or change lanes altogether while cornering. The incoming speed has locked the patrol car into just one line through the corner. The vehicle position in the corner or upon

With a late apex, the officer will turn into the roadway so he is closest to the inside (apex) about two-thirds of the way through the curve.

corner exit is impossible to change at maximum speeds.

It definitely is not the quickest nor safest way through a turn. In this situation, all the officer can do is hope to keep the car on the roadway, and hope that no obstacles appear that block the road or force a lane change.

In selecting proper position for a turn, the officer should attempt to drive the car through the line of minimum resistance to the vehicle, so that the officer is able to

With the late-apex method, the officer will see the corner exit before accelerating. He actually accelerates past the apex.

accelerate as early as possible and attain a maximum curve exit speed. It makes sense that the arc of the vehicle's path should be the sharpest where the speed is the slowest. This should be at the entry of the curve. The curve should be approached from the outside and the driver should hold this lane position late or deep into the turn.

While attempting to establish proper position or line through a curve, the driver should scan the curve while approaching. The path of travel should bring the vehicle to the apex or inside of the turn just prior to that time when the vehicle is pointed out of the turn. The length of time and distance at the apex depends on the radius of the turn. On a long sweeping turn it may be hundreds of feet. In tight turns only a few feet. The car should be held as close as possible to the apex to allow room when exiting the turn. The driver may then unwind the steering wheel and allow the car to smoothly drift out to the outside upon leaving the turn. The officer should attempt to exit in a way that will allow staying within the correct lane.

It should be noted, that if a curve is properly negotiated, the driver could, if necessary, exit the turn on either side of the roadway. This may be needed to establish proper entry position into a subsequent curve in the opposite direction. Generally speaking, entry speed and proper entry position are the key points to safe, fast cornering.

Most corners, even for race car drivers, are late apex corners. Most residential streets, street corners, intersections and side streets are all late apex. Start wide in your lane, and decrease the radius down smoothly to the inside edge of the corner. When you're two-thirds of the way around the corner, let the car come out at the exit.

The Handling Oval

The Bondurant Handling Oval is an important tool in teaching the basics of cornering. The handling oval is made up of a wide, constant radius turn and a hairpin, increasing radius turn connected by two short straights. It is here that each student comes to terms with the late apex, the early apex, and the hazards of doing each the wrong way. We practice car positioning into the turn, finding the braking point, hard straight-line braking, trail braking, hitting the apex or closest point to the inside of the turn, increasing throttle, and exit of the turn.

The handling oval is basically two 60-mile per hour straightaways. The straights end in an early apex corner on one end and a late apex corner on the other end. You accelerate down the straightaway on The Bondurant Handling Oval, lift off the gas and squeeze on the brake. Start turning in for the particular apex in that corner. The apex is not just one point of a corner or turn. It is an area of the inside of the corner that the car passes through. Then turn the wheel out to exit and squeeze on the gas.

The rule is to nearly always take a late apex into a turn. This technique is slower into the turn, since the braking is done ahead of time, but it is the fastest and most stable out of the turn. It allows an officer to place his squad anywhere on the road he wants to as he exits the corner instead of being forced to the outside to collide with oncoming traffic or to run off the road altogether. An early apex, or turning into the corner too soon, is the biggest reason for single-car accidents.

The late apex method is the safest cornering technique, allowing the officer to place the vehicle in any lane as he exits the corner. It is frequently also the fastest cornering technique.

Like all road surfaces wider than one car width, the handling oval has a "line" around it that is the fastest path. In terms of police work, this "line" is also sometimes the safest path. When in doubt about a corner, such as in an uncertain area or under uncertain weather conditions, a turn should be treated as a late apex corner. This means the corner should be approached wide, and the turn not be started until very late. This approach will allow the driver to either exit the turn wide or exit it tight. An early apex turn forces the car to go wide into possible road debris, lane blockage, or oncoming traffic.

Start turning into the corner and as soon as you turn, feel the weight transfer to the outside front wheel. That is when you start your trail braking. Gently ease off the brake. You are still braking a third of the way into the corner. You have more control that way. Pick up the throttle gently as you feel the weight transfer to the rear of the car.

As soon as you feel the car stabilize, then feed more throttle. As you pass through the apex of the corner, keep the front end tucked into the apex. When you can see the straightaway, that is where your exit starts. Gently unwind the wheel as you accelerate, just like on the Throttle Steer Circle. Unwind the steering wheel as more throttle is applied. Together, the weight transfer and the throttle will steer you to the exit and down the road.

The two most common driving technique errors made by a fleeing motorist are turning into a corner too soon and waiting too long to brake.

This driver has mistakenly turned into the corner too soon, taking an early apex. This is a common error for fleeing motorists and police officers alike.

It is very important to accelerate smoothly, rolling off the gas smoothly, smoothly squeezing on the brakes, controlling all the traction and the weight transfer of your car. As the driver, you are the one who controls the weight transfer and traction of the vehicle. Be smooth and you will always have traction. Be rough and abrupt with the steering, the brakes, and the acceleration, and sooner or later you will spin out.

Suppose you are doing 60 miles per hour in your squad car down the straightaway on the handling oval toward the late apex corner. It is time to roll off the gas pedal. The weight starts transferring forward onto the front shocks and springs, compressing down onto the tire patches.

With an early apex, the driver is to the inside of the corner before he can see through the corner.

The driver has waited too long to brake. By using an early apex, the driver can't stay in his own lane through the corner.

Now you start squeezing on the brakes. Think of both the throttle and brakes as big sponges. Squeeze on the brakes as if you are squeezing water out of a sponge, not stomping the brakes. Squeezing on them enables you to have a nice smooth, clean weight transfer forward. When you start turning into the corner, keep the brakes on. As soon as the front end takes you out then start trailing off the brake.

Trail off the brakes means start releasing brake pressure gradually until you are about halfway through the corner. Then pick up the throttle lightly, and feel the weight transfer to the rear and to the outside, stabilizing the car. Then squeeze on as much throttle as the car will take. Exit out of the corner long and wide. Make the car go where you want it to with the throttle.

Now you are approaching the early apex corner on the handling oval. A big difference exists on the line that you take through the corner. You are going to turn into the corner much earlier. The inside

wheel is going to pick up the inside of the corner much earlier. Trail brake all the way through the apex until you feel the car is settled. Squeeze on the throttle and accelerate, turning the car out long and wide.

Even under maximum cornering, an early apex and late braking force the car into oncoming traffic or off the road.

8
Enforcement Driving

During all emergency runs, the officer must use both the emergency lights and siren. The laws vary state to state and the policies vary agency to agency on which lights to use: lightbar, grille/deck, wig-wag headlights, front facing lights only, rear facing lights only, or combinations of these, depending on the stage of the run. However, SOME emergency lights must be used and so must the siren unless specifically directed otherwise by the dispatcher.

Most state statutes place two requirements on the driver of all public safety vehicles: (1) The officer must drive with due regard for the safety of all persons using the public streets and highways; (2) A public safety vehicle only gains or requests the right-of-way when using both the emergency lights and siren.

Upon approaching either a red traffic light or a stop sign, slow down in anticipation of cross traffic. As unrealistic as it may

Even with emergency lights and siren activated, as the officer approaches a red light or stop sign, he must slow down in anticipation of cross-traffic. Emergency lights do not grant the right-of-way. They only request it.

The green light does not give the officer the right to drive without due regard for the safety of others. Motorists turn right on red and oncoming motorists turn left on green.

seem to those trained by Hollywood-style pursuits, the officer must slow down enough at each of these intersections to be able to come to a complete stop before he crosses the intersection!

In urban situations, where a cross-traffic collision is likely, this means the officer will be under full throttle up to the intersection, followed by full braking as he approaches the intersection, then full throttle again to the next intersection. That is the hard way, but the only way to always operate with due regard for the safety of all others using the street or highway. Any other way and the officer will be liable.

The officer should not treat green lights as an opportunity to blow through the intersection at speed. Many motorists turn right on red after only a brief look to oncoming traffic. Many senior citizens underestimate the approach speed or the time to respond in simple traffic situations. Many motorists turn left in front of oncoming traffic. Some will turn left in front of a police car just as some will try to beat a train. After all, if your lights and siren are activated, you are already on some emergency business and are unlikely to stop that motorist for a simple failure to yield.

Failure of the officer to drive "with due regard" may be deemed "willful and

During routine patrol, under low stress, and at low speeds, this is what the officer sees. The officer is well aware of the car and truck traffic at the intersection. On emergency runs and during pursuits, the officer's peripheral vision is greatly reduced.

wanton" misconduct. The police officer simply cannot operate without due regard for the safety of others. This, in turn, leads many officers to discontinue a pursuit when they find themselves or the public exposed to high risk or unnecessary danger.

Overtaking Other Motorists

During an emergency response, you will overtake other cars as fast as if they were standing still, literally. A patrol car running 110 miles per hours, which is common, passing the general traffic flow driving 55 miles per hours, is the same as driving 55 miles per hour by a row of parked cars. Actually, it is more dangerous, since the patrol car running 110 miles per hour has four times the energy as the same car running 55 miles per hours. This energy must be dissipated by the brakes or by collapsing sheet metal.

The concern with driving 55 miles per hour past a row of parked cars is that one will suddenly pull onto the street. The same goes for a high-speed overtake of a line of traffic. One of the cars in the traffic flow may suddenly pull into your lane. The effect is the same: a 55-mile per hour impact. In overtake mode, the officer will almost certainly be concentrating on the violator he is trying to overtake, on finding a median crossover, or on what he will do once he arrives at his emergency destination.

The overtaking officer must be aware of the risks during overtake driving. This is especially true of the time the officer is closing the gap but has not yet activated his emergency lights. The motorist may check his mirrors but not recognize the cruiser as an emergency vehicle, nor realize how quickly the officer is overtaking traffic. In this case, more than ever, the officer is completely liable for any resulting accidents. Without his emergency lights and

As a result of increased speeds and stress, tunnel vision sets in and the officer sees less of what is around him. His focus is on the road in front of him or the fleeing driver. He may miss some of the traffic in and around this busy intersection.

Driving under extreme stress or at very high speeds is like driving with blinders on. The intersection of two major state roads looks like this to the officer. Peripheral vision is gone. The driver can fight this narrow band of vision by physically turning his head left and right.

siren activated, the officer is legally required to obey the posted speed limits. The rapid overtake of traffic, with or without warning gear activated, places a heavy burden on the officer to DRIVE DEFENSIVELY.

It is dangerous to pass traffic on the right when the emergency lights and siren are operating. The first reaction of motorists when they recognize you as an emergency vehicle is to pull to the right. You are running 90 miles per hour to overtake a speeder. The traffic is running 55 miles per hour. This means you are overtaking traffic at 50 feet per second. Motorists will typically not recognize your

police cruiser until you are 100 feet or so behind them. In the next two seconds, they will suddenly pull to the right just as you pass them on the right: a collision.

If you are passing on the right and a motorist runs you off the road, he or she is only complying with the law and yielding to an emergency vehicle. Give traffic a chance to get out of your way. If traffic won't yield to you, and it frequently won't, pass to the left if possible. If traffic won't yield and you can't pass to the left, your only available option is to shut off both red light and siren and cautiously go around them on the right.

Tunnel Vision

The first thing that happens to an officer in the stress of an emergency run is the loss of peripheral vision. The result is called "tunnel vision." The officer focuses only on a narrow width of the road ahead or on the fleeing violator and does not see things around the car in his peripheral vision. This is aggravated by a normal loss of peripheral vision as speeds increase.

Peripheral vision drops from a total band of 150 degrees at low speeds and no stress to a band of 120 degrees by 40 miles

Crossing a divided highway at the median strip requires the officer to slow from speeds over 100 miles per hour, with no braking reference points, to hit a narrow cross-over.

The key to hitting the narrow median strip during a U-turn is early braking. Nearly 100 percent of the braking is done in a straight line. Turn in under full control.

per hour. At 50 miles per hour this drops to 90 degrees, and by 60 miles per hour to just 60 degrees. At 80 miles per hour, the peripheral vision is just 30 degrees. This is like driving with blinders on, at just the time you need maximum vision to sweep intersections for oncoming traffic.

The best way to fight the effects of tunnel vision is to physically move your head back and forth. You cannot increase your peripheral vision nor break free of tunnel vision. You will have the same narrow field of view in the direction your eyes are looking. However, by forcing yourself to sweep your head left and right, you are able to see more of the surroundings. Think of it as having blinders or wearing a snow parka hood pulled tight. Your eyes will not move, practically speaking. To see what tunnel vision is hiding from you, simply move your head, and your eyes will follow.

U-Turns

A big part of traffic enforcement involves clocking oncoming vehicles with moving radar. The police car traveling at highway speeds in one direction must slow down, turn around, accelerate, and overtake a speeder moving in the opposite direction. The U-turn done by the officer varies by the kind of road being patrolled.

On a two-lane road, the technique is simply to brake hard while still on the roadway, then pull onto the right-hand shoulder. Depending on the lane width, the turning radius of the patrol car, and the condition of the shoulder, the officer may put two or four wheels on the shoulder. From the right-hand shoulder, a hand-over-hand full lock of the wheel will allow the cruiser to turn on the tightest radius. As proven by the Bondurant Throttle Steer Circle, the LEAST throttle applied during the turn allows for the tightest turn. Once the police vehicle has turned completely around and both drive tires have traction, full throttle can be applied.

The turning circle, curb to curb, for the 1999 Ford Police Interceptor, for example, is 40.9 feet. The width of an average, two-lane state highway, from white line to white line, is 22 feet. In most cases, the shoulder must be used. Just enough throttle to get through the turn will require the least amount of shoulder. The back end of the cruiser can indeed be spun around using the throttle. However, the traction-control/traction-assist must be deactivated first.

If the shoulders will not allow a U-turn, the other two options are a two-point turn and a three-point turn. The two-point turn involves pulling nose first (left-hand side) or backing (right-hand side) into a road or driveway, then pulling back out on the road facing the other direction.

Both versions of this turn involve backing in reverse in the driving lane. This is a risk. Backing into a roadway, after pulling in nose-first, increases the risk of a rear-end collision. Backing into a side road or driveway, in preparation to pull out nose first, increases the risk of missing the drive and getting stuck. It is very easy to lose control of the car or collide with unseen objects when backing.

The three-point turn is the least preferred method of making a U-turn. This should be used only when the road and shoulders are too narrow for a U-turn, and there are no nearby side roads to allow a two-point turn. Pull the car to the right as far as you can, turn the steering wheel full lock to the left, and give the cruiser just enough throttle to cross both lanes. Then shift into reverse, turn the wheel full lock to the right, and back up. Shift into drive, straighten the wheels, and slowly accelerate. The three-point turn is the slowest and highest risk method of making a U-turn. The cruiser is across both lanes of traffic for most of the maneuver, and the turn takes more than 10 seconds to perform. Sometimes there is no other choice.

Crossing Median Strips

On a multiple lane road with two or more lanes moving in opposite directions, an officer may have two choices when performing a U-turn. One is to cross the grassy median at the paved crossover spots. This narrow strip requires that the cruiser slow down to under 20 miles per hour, turn onto the median crossover, then pull back onto the other lanes. The trick here is to decelerate from extremely high speeds and hit a strip typically just two car-widths wide.

The late apex method allows the officer to accelerate as soon as the vehicle hits the median strip. Unlike racing, the officer should also be prepared to stop right here.

The officer is now giving the cruiser full throttle, but is remaining in his own traffic lane.

This narrow margin for error requires the officer to do all the braking in a straight line and be very careful not to overshoot the median crossover! With little traffic, the officer may pull into the driving lane (or the Number 2 or 3 lane) and then turn across the passing lane (Number 1 lane) onto the median. This will make the radius of the corner much larger and allow faster speeds and trail braking. However, the officer cannot carry so much speed into the median crossover that he cannot stop for oncoming traffic.

The stop from 100 miles per hour or more to under 20 miles per hour to make a tight right-angle turn onto a narrow center strip is much more difficult than anything a race car driver does. Racers have numerous braking reference points or brake markers before the turns. Not so on Interstate 75. If a racer brakes too late, he simply runs wide on the corner exit. He may even hang a wheel off the track. Not so for the police officer. If he brakes too late for the median crossover, he could very well end up in a drainage ditch.

Crossing the Median

For two years in a row, I wrote more traffic citations than any other officer in the county. Most of these involved crossing a median to apprehend a speeder. I had the median crossing technique down pat, regardless of weather. No median was too steep. No median was too muddy. In fact, my cruiser always had mud and grass hanging off the rear quarter panels and rear bumper, a badge of honor. The sheriff has occasionally made notes on my log book like, "This is not a TRACTOR, keep it out of the MEDIAN." I was not completely convinced he was serious. After all, I hadn't met a median yet that I couldn't jump in total confidence.

I clocked an oncoming blue 1996 Bonneville SSE running 89 miles per hour in a 55-mile per hour zone. I locked the radar reading, got on the brakes hard, and entered the median at a very shallow angle. This median had been a challenge in the past. It had a steep incline down, then a waterway, then a raised area, then another waterway, then a very steep incline up to the oncoming lanes. The median was 100 yards wide and, at the time, had standing water in the waterways with the whole median covered with wet, slushy snow.

As I reached the bottom of the first incline, I hit the gas. Momentum is the key. I sailed through the first waterway, over the rise and through the second waterway, running about 60 miles per hour. Then the ground fell out from under me. With a jolt and a loud THUD, I crossed a 1-foot deep, 6-foot wide culvert, hidden by snow and grass.

The impact put me into a broadside slide up the incline. I had spun around too far to correct for the slide and lost too much momentum to reach the top of the incline. I was stuck for the first time in my police career. I tried to rock the car but each motion took the car farther down the steep incline into the watery abyss.

No problem. I had a car phone. I would call the wrecker to pull me up onto the pavement, pay cash, and the sheriff would never know. Then I noticed the pegged temperature gauge and smelled the antifreeze. The impact had popped a freeze plug out of the block. I would have to be towed all the way back to the department. No problem. I'll fix it myself on Sunday and act totally innocent on Monday.

Then the police radio broke the silence, and my plan, with a message covering five counties: "Unit 4-8, the 10-51 (tow truck) is now 10-76 (en route) to your location." As a courtesy, the tow truck service called the sheriff's department to confirm their estimated time of arrival, and the dispatcher dutifully relayed it.

Of course, along with the tow truck were three squad cars driven by bored and nosy cops, wondering why I needed a tow truck since there was no dispatch of an accident. My uniformed cheering section did not need to tell the sheriff. He, too, heard the radio broadcast. I am still not completely convinced he meant everything he said the next day.

—Corporal Ed Sanow
Benton County, Indiana,
Sheriff's Department

The key to successfully crossing a grassy median strip is a shallow approach angle. This prevents both damage to the front facia and getting stuck by being high-centered.

If the median is muddy, the officer must carry quite a bit of speed into it.

Splish. Splash. Now is the time to keep the wheels straight and give the cruiser some gas. If you brake here, you will get stuck.

Once the left front wheel reaches pavement, turn hard and brake. A blip of the throttle will probably bring the rear end right around.

Not even the tightest race track hairpin forces the race car to slow down from its top speed to just 15 miles per hour. But that is exactly what a median crossing involves for the police officer.

All of this points to early braking as the key to quickly and consistently crossing the median. Nearly 100 percent of the braking for a median will be in a straight line. Get all of the braking done, down to very slow speeds, then turn into the median under full control. The safest way is to brake hard for the right angle turn and begin to accelerate as the turn is started. In most cases, the officer will be forced to conduct all of the setup for the turn inside his own driving lane. The exit will also be inside the passing lane.

The other method commonly used by traffic officers is to simply drive through the grassy median strip, do a U-turn, and end up facing the other direction on the other side of the median. While this median jumping is so common as to literally define a traffic officer, very real hazards are also common.

One is getting stuck in the median, because it is too wet, muddy, sandy, or snowy. Another is vehicle damage from debris in the median or hazards hidden by the grass. Another risk is getting high centered and either stuck or damaging the vehicle or both due to the steep sides of the median. Both risks are embarrassing beyond description. The two keys to successful median crossing are high incoming speeds and very shallow incoming angles. The high crossing speed, 35 to 50 miles per hour, will allow the cruiser enough momentum to cross even a low traction median and reach the high traction of the opposite side shoulder. In fact, the officer may slow to 35 miles per hour, turn into the median, and then accelerate to get to the other side. Under very low traction conditions, the cruiser may actually enter the opposite side of the road facing the oncoming traffic. Typically, however, the cruiser will end up perpendicular to the oncoming traffic as he completes the U-turn. Either way, a blip of the throttle has the cruiser pointed in the correct direction and ready to overtake the violator.

The angle of entry into the median should be very shallow, very gradual. If you are going to sink up to your floorboards in a soggy median, you want to be near your own shoulder, not cross-wise in the median. More importantly, the shallow approach will allow you to drive down the side of even very steep medians. This is especially the case for medians with drain channels to handle both sides of the road, where the center of the median actually rises up. A very shallow approach will allow the cruiser to cross even a steep median with no ground clearance problems. The cruiser should enter the median at a shallow angle, and continue at this shallow angle across the median. Don't try to turn sharply on the grass moving at high speed. The cruiser simply doesn't have the traction, and the car will simply understeer. You do not want to reach the shoulder and pavement on the other side with your wheels turned sharply in an understeer mode. This is especially true if the shoulder or pavement has a slight drop off onto the median, or if the median has a hidden hole or rut. This can cause severe wheel, tire, and alignment damage.

If you have carried a lot of speed through the median, it may take both of the oncoming traffic lanes to slow down and turn around.

In the worst case, the officer may need to use the far shoulder of the oncoming traffic lane to make the U-turn.

The steeper the side of the median or the sharper the "V" at the bottom of the median, the shallower the driving angle should be. A shallow angle keeps the cruiser from getting high centered and from dragging bumpers, air deflectors, or facia as the median cross is made. Medians that cannot be crossed at a 90 degree angle in a 4x4 Explorer can be easily be crossed at a 5 degree angle in a low-slung Camaro and Crown Victoria.

Once the left front wheel is on the opposite side shoulder, a turn of the wheel and hard braking will pull the back end around while a transition to the throttle will keep it coming around. The cruiser literally spins around, pivoting off the left front tire.

As the median quality gets worse in terms of traction, wait longer and longer to brake. In some cases, slow somewhat to enter, accelerate all the way through the median, and brake only on the pavement on the other side. This, of course, requires the oncoming traffic lanes to be OPEN. The cruiser must brake and U-turn starting from facing the wrong way on the passing lane shoulder for the oncoming traffic. This technique is used for slippery conditions when the tires will be wet, snowy, or muddy enough to allow the back end to be easily spun around.

In the worst case, the cruiser may run from the oncoming passing lane shoulder to the oncoming driving lane shoulder in order to make the U-turn. Even under dry conditions where the cruiser can get turned around using just the median, shoulder, and passing lane, pay attention to oncoming traffic in the driving lane. Even though you know what you are doing, they may not know and may panic. They may unexpectedly pull into the passing lane.

Intersections

The toughest and yet most common corner a police officer faces is the simple 90-degree intersection. It has no smooth run-off area. No tire wall. On most state and county roads, one two-way road intersects another two-way road, with one 11-foot wide lane intersecting another 11-foot wide lane at a right angle.

No need to worry about where the apex is or what the best line through the corner is. No need to worry about how much speed to carry through the corner. It's simple. You must slow from 55 miles per hour or 110 miles per hour to just 20 miles per hour. Don't try to see how fast you can come into a right angle, intersecting corner. Instead, see how fast you can exit it. See how little of the oncoming lane you use. That is the essence of a late apex turn. All the braking is done BEFORE you reach the apex and you accelerate past the apex.

One of the most important aspects of high-speed vehicle control is what auto racers call the "line." The line is the fastest path around a road course. This means the proper lane positioning for the fastest entry onto a straightaway and the proper lane positioning for the hardest braking into a corner. However, in police work, officer safety and vehicle control are more important than sheer speed.

The two most common driving errors are turning into a corner too soon and coming into a corner too fast. As a result, officers should be taught early, conservative braking in a straight line. Most of the braking should be done well ahead of the turn. Officers should also be taught to delay turning into the corner until they can see completely through the turn. This late apex technique is the safest overall, gives the officer the most options as he completes the

The turnaround made famous by Bob Bondurant student James Garner is called the Reverse 180 Degree Spin. Come to a stop. Shift into reverse. Crank the wheel hard to the left. *Rick Scuteri*

Accelerate hard in reverse until the car crosses the center line. Don't touch the brakes. *Rick Scuteri*

Suddenly lift off the gas. This will transfer weight from the front to the rear. The front end will slide around. Shift from reverse to drive. *Rick Scuteri*

As the front end slides around, crank the steering wheel straight, then to the right. You are ready to accelerate away. *Rick Scuteri*

turn and, ironically, is the fastest in the long run.

In addition to the fastest exit speed, late apex cornering is also the safest method in giving the most vehicle control. It also gives the driver the most accident avoidance options as he exits the turn. By driving the "technically correct" line, the officer can overtake violators in faster and better-handling cars.

180 Spins

Let's talk about forward and reverse 180 spins. What's the purpose of them? Say you are going down the road and someone goes screaming by in the other direction, someone you need to apprehend. You need to quickly stop and turn around. You can do this by the forward 180 spin. This is the so-called "bootleg" 180 degree turn involving the emergency brake and sliding the rear end of the cruiser around.

To set up for a forward 180 degree spin, brake from highway speeds down to about 25 or 30 miles per hour. It only takes a half of a turn of the steering wheel to the left to make a forward 180 degree spin to the left. At 25 miles per hour, jam on the emergency brake as you turn the wheel to the left. Get ready to release the emergency brake with your left hand. As soon as you have come up on 180 degrees, release the emergency brake, and accelerate smoothly.

It can be tough to release the emergency brake while steering, depending upon where the release is. Some emergency foot brakes pump to set and then pump to release. The officer with an awkwardly located brake release will want to practice this technique a lot.

Front-wheel drive cars, like this Taurus SHO, can indeed be driven very aggressively. Front-drive cars almost never oversteer when driven near the limit.

When pushed hard, a front-wheel drive car may understeer, like this Taurus SHO. Cadence braking is one solution. Cadence throttle is another solution. Unlike rear-drive cars, front-drive cars almost always go where the front wheels are pointed.

Let's talk about a reverse 180 spin, the maneuver made famous by James Garner (a Bondurant graduate) on the TV series, *The Rockford Files.* Come to a stop at a slight angle, with the nose facing slightly toward the shoulder. Just as the car comes to a stop, shift into reverse, take your foot off the brake, and accelerate backward. Try not to spin the tires because you will lose time. You want to back rapidly toward the center line. Once the rear bumper crosses the center line at a 45 degree angle, suddenly lift off the gas. Weight will transfer from the front tires to the rear tires leaving the front tire patches very small.

Do not use the brakes for this technique. Do not touch the emergency brakes or the brake pedal. Just accelerate hard backward and suddenly lift off the gas. Crank the steering wheel hard a full lock to the left. That will cause the front of the car to spin around to the right avoiding oncoming traffic. Halfway around the slide, shift from reverse to first gear as you straighten the front wheels up. That will put you around in a perfect reverse 180 and ready to accelerate away.

9

Pursuit Driving and Decisions

We have had police pursuits long before we have had police cars. In the Old West, the sheriff would round up the posse and ride off into the sunset in pursuit of the bandits. No one questioned whether or not to pursue. The question of how long to pursue was simply a matter of supplies. Today that is like pursuing until the patrol car runs out of gas.

Starting in the 1980s, many police departments began to question whether to pursue at all. Public and political reaction to tragic third-party deaths as a result of police pursuits became intense. It was acceptable for the violator to hurt himself when fleeing. It was regrettable when an officer got hurt during a pursuit. However, it was totally unacceptable for an innocent and uninvolved bystander to be injured or killed. The whole process of pursuit driving was called into question.

Police departments reacted in a number of ways. Some departments adopted "no pursuit" or severely restricted pursuit

Traffic permitting, the half-lane straddle allows oncoming traffic to see some of the emergency lights. These lights may be blocked if the cruiser is directly behind the violator.

The half-lane straddle gives the officer a better view of what is ahead, both traffic and obstacles. The half-lane straddle can also have an intimidating effect on the fleeing motorist.

policies. Many departments shifted the authority to continue the pursuit away from the involved officer and to a supervisor. The departments that allowed unrestricted or officer-discretion pursuits provided a checklist or series of questions for the officer to assist his decision making. Many more departments provided low-speed training in vehicles for the first time. Officers patrolling in the special service package Ford Mustang and Chevrolet Camaro received high-speed training in addition to low-speed Emergency Vehicle Operation Course (EVOC) training.

Lethal Force Guidelines

The use of lethal force to apprehend a fleeing felon was the subject of the United Sates Supreme Court decision in *Tennessee v. Garner* (1985). In this case, an officer shot a fleeing felon that he could not outrun on foot. The Court established a number of guidelines for the use of lethal force against fleeing felons. It just so happens these

guidelines work very well for the use of pursuits to apprehend a fleeing driver.

As a guideline, for the use of lethal force to be justified by the courts: (1) the person fleeing must have committed a violent, forcible felony against another person; and (2) this fact is known to you beyond a reasonable doubt; and (3) his escape now means he will be free indefinitely; and (4) all other means of capture have been exhausted; and (5) his continued freedom represents a clear and present danger to the life of other persons.

This is certainly not the standard for the start of a pursuit. However, it must be quickly considered as the pursuit continues and especially as the forcible end of the pursuit is considered.

This is the basis for some departments banning pursuits for traffic infractions and misdemeanors. This is also the basis for a arguable presumption that the registered owner of the vehicle is the driver. This allows the police to run the license plate

This is a six-car pile-up just waiting to happen. Even though this is what you see in real pursuits from TV news helicopters, DON'T DO THIS. Spread out. Everyone should have a four-second gap.

number, break off the pursuit, and arrest the owner at a later time. This is also the basis for trying all other options: rolling roadblocks, tire deflating devices, and stationary roadblocks.

It is also the reasoning behind most pursuit strategies of profound patience as long as the fleeing driver does not present a real danger to other persons. This means the police will follow the violator for many miles and many minutes as long as he remains on the interstate. As soon as the violator exits to endanger densely populated areas, he is instantly forced out by vehicle impacts or gunfire. Both vehicular impacts and firearms are considered lethal force.

The Deadly Statistics

Far from the image cast by Hollywood, the police pursuit is extremely dangerous duty. In fact, one out of three pursuits initiated for traffic infractions ends in an accident. When the pursuit is initiated for felony reasons, two out of three end in collisions because both the officer and the suspect take more chances.

One out of eight pursuits ends in an injury according to detailed studies by the California Highway Patrol and the Metro-Dade (Florida) Police. An average of 1 out of 100 pursuits ends in a death. These accidents can involve the officer, the fleeing suspect, or an innocent third party who just happens to be in the wrong place at the wrong time. Municipalities pay out more in liability claims related to the police vehicle than all other forms of liability combined, including firearms.

Of the police officers who die in the line of duty, 49 percent are killed by gunfire. However, 38 percent, the second largest category, die as a result of a traffic accident while on routine patrol, during an emergency response or while in pursuit.

During a pursuit or a tense emergency response, the body undergoes some significant psychological and physiological changes (e.g. tunnel vision, time and space distortions).

Police chiefs and sheriffs are aware of this ongoing problem. However, with a limited training budget, firearms training tends to receive more emphasis. The perception is that everyone knows how to drive, but few know how and when to shoot. All that changed in 1989 when the Supreme Court handed down its landmark decision in *City of Canton, Ohio, v. Harris.*

The Court said a department that fails to train its people in all tasks performed as a normal part of their job can be found "deliberately indifferent," which is a civil rights violation, according to U.S.C.A. Title 42, Section 1983. The Court wants to see a policy for: emergency and pursuit driving, the policy followed on a daily basis, and proof of training to meet the policy.

The high-speed pursuit is one of the most dangerous activities performed by a law enforcement officer. In fact, pursuit driving is a long series of life-or-death decisions. Between 6,000 and 8,000 pursuits per year end in crashes: the officer into a third party, the violator into a third party, the officer into the violator, the violator by himself, or the officer by himself.

These pursuit-related crashes injure 2,500 to 5,000 people per year. According to NHTSA, the traffic deaths declined from 51,091 in 1980 to 44,529 in 1990. However, the number of people killed in high-speed police pursuits has remained nearly constant. Between 240 and 330 people per year are killed in pursuit-related accidents.

Pursuits should not be viewed as challenging, exciting, or competition. Instead police officers should view pursuits for exactly what they really are: an extreme use of force with a continuous series of life-and-death decisions that risk the life of the officer, the violator, and innocent bystanders. There are no good pursuits. The best pursuit is no pursuit. Second best is a short one. The Phoenix Police Department determined that if its officers have not apprehended a fleeing driver within 90 seconds after the pursuit starts, the pursuit will end in some kind of accident.

In 1983, the California Highway Patrol conducted a six-month study of 683 pursuits on freeways. The study found the "average" pursuit will be initiated by a traffic violation; occur at night; continue for one mile; last two minutes; involve two police cars; be terminated voluntarily by the fleeing driver; and involve a male driver, 20 years old.

In 1984, the Metro-Dade (Florida), Police conducted a 12-month study of 398 pursuits in an urban environment. When combined with the 1983 California Highway Patrol study of 683 pursuits in freeway scenarios, the results are:

Reason for the pursuit: traffic infraction, 61 percent; be on lookout for, 13 percent; suspected felons, 9 percent; DUI and reckless driving, 4 percent; other, 13 percent. Length of the pursuit: under 5 minutes, 78 percent; 5 to 10 minutes, 16 percent; more than 10 minutes, 4 percent. Length of the

One out of three pursuits ends in an accident. One out of eight ends with an injury. A larger gap will give the officer more time to react to the violator and more of a chance to drive the correct line.

The secondary pursuit cars should be as far behind the lead pursuit car as the lead pursuit car is behind the fleeing car. Many departments wisely forbid more than three police cars in a pursuit: one primary unit and two secondary units.

average pursuit: 3 minutes. Results of the pursuit: resulted in accident, 30 percent; resulted in injuries, 12 percent; resulted in death, 1 percent. Breakdown of those injured in pursuits: driver or passenger in fleeing vehicle, 71 percent; police officer, 21 percent; uninvolved third party, 8 percent. Pursuits forcibly terminated by officer: 8 percent. Suspects apprehended as a result of a pursuit: 72 percent.

Deciding To Pursue

Before initiating the pursuit and all throughout the pursuit, police officers and their supervisors should ask themselves a number of questions. What is the offense involved? Is it a traffic infraction? Misdemeanor? Felony? Does the purpose of the pursuit warrant the risks involved? What is the nature and seriousness of the suspected offense? Is the fleeing motorist suspected of committing a serious crime or only a misdemeanor? Is the motorist already operating his vehicle in a reckless and life-threatening manner, or has he only committed a minor traffic violation? Is there a need for immediate apprehension? Is the fleeing driver known to the officer, so an arrest can be made on a warrant at a later date?

If the officer knows, or should have known, that the fleeing vehicle is operated by

a juvenile who has committed a misdemeanor or nonviolent felony, strong consideration should be given to cutting off the pursuit if it lasts for more than a minute or so.

What are the road and weather conditions? Is it sunny and dry or raining at night? Visibility should be considered. Bright sun or fog makes it difficult for other motorists to see the flashing warning lights on an approaching police vehicle. What is the condition of the roadway? What type of road surface is it? Loose gravel or paved road? Is the road surface wet, slick, icy, or sandy?

What are the performance characteristics and general state of repair of the police vehicles involved and are they capable of traveling safely at a high rate of speed? Have the pursuit vehicles been inspected to ensure that they do not have dangerously worn shocks, tires, or brakes that grab during hard braking? What is the condition of the police vehicle? Is it brand new and in great condition? Or is it nearing its mandatory retirement with nearly 100,000 miles on it?

Is the lead pursuit car up to the task? Does the police car have enough horsepower to actually overtake the violator? Or will the police cruiser be pushed to or beyond its limits just to keep the fleeing vehicle in

Accidents happen at intersections and on curves, not on straight, flat roads. The time to use the radio is when steering skills are NOT needed. Also try to avoid using the radio when cresting a hill or when overtaking heavy traffic.

sight? What vehicle are you in? A V-6-powered midsize police sedan is no match for a high-performance sports car. According to their manufacturer, the sport-utes are not to be used for enforcement-class pursuit and emergency driving, specifically the four-wheel drive Chevrolet Tahoe, all Ford Expeditions, and all Ford Explorers.

Are you a officer on a motorcycle? The motorcycle officer really should not be in a high-speed pursuit. Among other things, the motorcycle offers no cover or protection. It puts the officer in a dangerous situation against drivers who are not reacting properly or fast enough to emergency signals. It also is a vehicle that has

To Pursue Or Not Pursue?

To pursue or not pursue, that is the question. But is there a correct, compact answer? No! It is, however, in the best interest of police agencies and public safety for police administrators to address the question of pursuits and to establish a clear pursuit policy.

Let's deal with the obvious question first. Should police agencies ever engage in vehicular pursuits? There is a safe option, at least safe for the police, when it comes to pursuits: Do not allow officers to engage in pursuits. To prescribe such a policy nationwide, as some people demand, would be contrary and disastrous to public safety.

Here are some facts I would like you to mull over: Each year in this country, some 50,000 people lose their lives because of traffic accidents. Almost 50 percent of those fatalities involve drunk drivers. If officers never pursued the 1.7 million drunken drivers arrested in this country each year, how many more traffic deaths would occur? I suggest to you that that number would far exceed the number of deaths that result from pursuits.

Approximately 25 percent of the California Highway Patrol's (CHP) pursuits involved drunk drivers. Should officers not attempt to stop the drunk on the wrong side of the road or driving at a high speed through stop signs? I think not! I find that concept irresponsible.

Ah, but what about chasing after a car with a burned-out taillight or headlight or similar "minor" infraction, because the driver will not pull over? Well, here are a few examples that address just such cases:

Ted Bundy was apprehended in Florida after a police pursuit initiated because of a license plate violation. How many more young women would

Bundy have killed if he had not been pursued and arrested that night?

Randy Kraft was recently convicted in California of murdering 16 young men. He was arrested by CHP officers when they stopped him for lane straddling and subsequently found a murdered Marine in his car. Had Kraft elected not to pull over and the officers were prohibited from pursuing him, how many more murders might have occurred?

I remember one particular chase I was involved in as a young officer. I attempted to stop a car for a taillight violation. The driver would not pull over, and so my partner and I pursued him. When we finally got the driver to stop, we found out why he fled: there were four men in the car armed with sawed-off shotguns and a knife. They had all raped a young woman and were in the process of attempting to murder her with a knife when we initiated the stop.

The woman lived. But what would have happened had we not pursued the car?

Literally thousands of stolen vehicles are recovered each year because of pursuits that started out as traffic stops. Every day in this country, numerous arrests are made for transporting large quantities of illicit drugs. Many of these arrests begin when an officer attempts to stop a person for traffic violation, the driver flees, and the officer pursues.

Criminals fleeing violent crimes, such as armed robbery, frequently come to the attention of an officer because of a traffic violation, but the officer has no knowledge of the original crime. How many of these violent criminals would escape if the officers did not pursue?

—Maury Hannigan, Commissioner (ret.)
California Highway Patrol

The driver of the lead pursuit car is under incredible stress. For the safety of the pursuit, the second pursuit car, in this case the all-white cruiser, should handle as much of the pursuit communication as possible.

less conspicuous warning lights and a weaker siren.

What is the location of the pursuit now? Will the pursuit take place on, or move to, residential streets, a business district, a freeway, or narrow country-type roads? Is it a narrow single-lane road with steep shoulders? Or a wide, dual-lane with generous shoulders and run-off areas? Consider the number of curves and hills and the number of potential blind spots. Consider the number of intersections and driveways where other vehicles could suddenly and unexpectedly enter. Same for the use of

The police officer should focus on one of two places: what is well ahead of the fleeing car or what is happening in the gap between the cruiser and the fleeing car. The pursuit is approaching the most dangerous intersection in the county. Do not visually lock on the violator's taillights.

the roadway by pedestrians and bicyclists. What is the environment of the pursuit? Is it through heavy traffic in an urban area? Light traffic in a rural area?

Where is the pursuit headed? Out to an interstate or rural area or instead into a densely populated area? Are you familiar with the roads in the direction the pursuit is headed? Any special dangers ahead? Curves? Intersections? Is the pursuit area congested with vehicular traffic and pedestrians or is traffic density light, making it reasonable to assume that other vehicles or pedestrians will hear the warning signal of an approaching police vehicle and yield the right of way?

Is air support available? Once the helicopter arrives at the scene, the pursuing units need to back off and let the aircraft run the pursuit. Too often the ground units continue to press the fleeing vehicle. When the police press harder, the tendency is for the fleeing vehicle to run harder. The result is most likely a collision. Back way off. Let the aircraft call in the pursuit. Follow at a safe distance. Let the fleeing driver concentrate more on driving and less on the pursuit cars. He will not outrun the helicopter.

When an aircraft is available and has visual contact with the pursued vehicle, the primary officer will generally discontinue the high-speed pursuit, allowing the aircraft to continue the surveillance of the suspect vehicle. The aircraft will assume the responsibility of directing the ground officers so as to apprehend the suspect without the dangers involved in a ground pursuit. Can you get additional police cruisers to help you? Can you get air support? Can a rolling roadblock be set up? Can stop sticks be used? Can a path be cleared ahead of the violator to let him safely pass through dangerous intersections?

Some pursuits are known to have covered 300 miles, cross three state lines, and involve dozens of different city, county, and state law enforcement officers. However, the AVERAGE pursuit is over in three minutes. This means helicopter air support is very unlikely. While a second responding unit is possible in an urban jurisdiction, more than two patrol cars being involved is also unlikely. This also means a rolling roadblock is unlikely. With the average pursuit over in three minutes, the use of stop sticks or other tire deflating devices is also unlikely. For the average pursuit, this means the pursuing officer will not have any outside help. It will be up to the officer to apprehend the fleeing driver.

What are your departmental policies? If you violate your department policies, the department may not defend you in the event of injury, death, and property damage. You will be personally responsible for civil litigation and personally responsible for any court judgment that comes as a result of the inevitable law suit. Even if the pursuit ends without incident, violating the department policy may result in being demoted or fired. Violation of the department policy is the very first piece of hard evidence that you disregarded the safety of others and operated a vehicle without due regard. That is a violation of state law.

Think these things out ahead of time. Learn to weigh them in your mind before you ever get involved in a pursuit. Practice running down a checklist of decisions. I will terminate a pursuit "IF". . . I will terminate a pursuit "WHEN". . .

Pursuit Techniques

The police emergency run from point A to point B is like solo racing, a.k.a. autocross. The police officer is alone with few outside influences. He will face traffic in all directions, of course, but generally controls how fast he drives, when he uses the mike, where he turns, when he stops, and how hard he accelerates, brakes, and takes corners.

The police pursuit is different from emergency driving. The officer is now following and trying to apprehend a driver in front of him. The pursuit is much more like a wheel-to-wheel race. Lessons from the race track apply to pursuit driving in a couple of areas. First, the pressure is on the fleeing driver in the lead car from the police officer in the trailing car. This kind of pressure can cause the fleeing motorist to push his car or abilities beyond their limits. That is bad for the fleeing driver.

During the pursuit, concentrate on driving the technically correct line, specifically on early braking and a late apex. The Jaguar has turned into the corner too soon (an early apex) and is braking hard. The deputy has braked early, held to the outside, and is getting ready to accelerate.

Calling Off the Pursuit

Whitestown Deputy Marshal Rick Hutchison was on routine patrol on a clear and bright afternoon. The Boone County, Indiana, Sheriff's dispatcher advised all units of a Buick station wagon being driven recklessly by a young female in the Whitestown area. A 14-year-old girl had persuaded her 16-year-old boyfriend to let her drive his parents' car.

Moments later, the Buick drove into Whitestown, spinning rubber, throwing gravel, and turning "donuts." Whitestown Marshal Keith Jones went to the center of town and got out of his patrol car to ask some questions, just as the Buick reached town. Marshal Jones, now on foot, radioed deputy Hutchison that the Buick was at the center of town. He stepped to the road to wave the Buick down and was nearly run over. The Buick then cut off to a side street, spraying the marshal with gravel and dirt. Less than 30 seconds later, the deputy marshal spotted the Buick. The pursuit was on, north out of town on County Road 650.

It was a 3-mile run to State Route 32. During this time, Hutchison, in his 1988 Caprice, was not able to gain on the Buick enough to read the license plate.

The fleeing Buick ran the stop sign at State Route 32. The road jogged and the Buick did not. It ended up in the front yard of a farm house and spun deep tracks in the yard getting back onto State Route 32 running east. This section of State Route 32 rises and falls with short but steep hills and dips in the road. The road has sections where a car easily disappears below the line of sight. The double yellow center line runs for miles.

Hutchison observed the Buick cross the double yellow line to pass a car at the bottom of a dip. Then he observed the Buick crossing the double yellow while cresting a hill to pass another car. This time, the Buick nearly hit an oncoming semi truck. Each violation was radioed in. As the pursuit continued, Hutchison became more concerned about the risks of continuing. The original offense was a traffic infraction, not a misdemeanor nor felony. The fleeing driver was an inexperienced driver, driving in an extremely reckless manner, and showing no sign of letting up.

For his part, Hutchison was in the much older of the two patrol cars and was concerned about the condition of the shocks, brakes, and tires at speeds well over 100 miles per hour. He radioed to the marshal that the pursuit was getting too crazy for him. He thought if he backed off, the young fleeing driver would also back off and take fewer risks. Hutchison was no faint-hearted wimp afraid of high speeds—in fact, he had extensive experience as an amateur dirt track racer. If the pursuit made someone of his experience uneasy, then it must have been risky indeed. Instead of timidity, Hutchison demonstrated maturity.

The marshal was closing the gap to his deputy but was still a few miles behind. He sensed both the risk of the situation and the subtle request to call off the pursuit. He radioed back since the risks were getting too high, to discontinue the pursuit. He then radioed the Boone County Sheriff's dispatch, which had already recorded that car-to-car traffic, "we are terminating the pursuit."

Hutchison turned off his emergency gear and slowed to patrol speeds. Three to four miles after he terminated the pursuit he came upon the accident he had hoped would not happen. The driver of the Buick had attempted to turn right on a gravel county road. Instead, the station wagon missed the turn, exited the road, became airborne, and crashed head first into a drainage ditch. The back end of the wagon came up in the air, ejecting the two kids out the tailgate, according to witnesses. The wagon then flipped over and landed on its top. Both occupants were unconscious. The boy broke his neck. The mother of the driver filed papers with the court declaring her intent to sue the town of Whitestown for causing the accident.

A copy of the dispatch audiotape, which contained the particulars of the reckless driving and the termination of the pursuit, changed her mind. This is a lesson in having a written policy, following the written policy, having an audio or video record of the event, and the willingness to call off a pursuit when the risks get too high.

—*Deputy Marshal Rick Hutchison,*
Whitestown, Indiana, Police
—*Marshal Keith Jones,*
Whitestown, Indiana, Police

Second, the "line" driven by the fleeing driver in the lead car will almost certainly affect the "line" driven by the police officer, whether or not that line was the best one. That is bad for the pursuing officer. The officer must concentrate on driving his car under control and with the proper braking and turning techniques, and not let the fleeing motorist dictate the "line."

The proper position for the lead pursuit vehicle is straddled a half-lane over to the left of the violator. This does three things. First, it allows oncoming traffic to see some of the emergency lights from the cruiser: one set of wig-wag headlights and half a lightbar. Both of these warning signals can be blocked by following directly behind a vehicle as tall as a pickup truck or minivan, even if the cruiser is equipped with a lightbar. The half-lane straddle will give traffic well ahead of the pursuit at least some idea of what is going on. They may not be able to tell a traffic stop from an on-going pursuit, but at least they are warned an enforcement vehicle is in the area.

The second reason for the lane straddle to the left is the effect on the fleeing driver.

He will see the cruiser, with all lights activated, through both the rear view mirror and the side mirror. This gives a sense of the cruiser being everywhere the driver looks. While he can easily deflect the rear view mirror, the outside mirror will produce a steady image of the cruiser. The half-lane straddle will give the fleeing driver the sense that the cruiser is overtaking or ready to pass at will, even if the cruiser holds a constant gap.

Third, the half-lane straddle gives the officer a better view of what is up ahead. He needs to be looking 10 car lengths ahead of the violator, and can't do that if he is directly behind the violator. A half-lane over, he will be able to see oncoming traffic, traffic moving in the same direction, and upcoming obstacles and intersections.

Using Lights and Siren

The law in all 50 states allows a police officer to disregard many traffic laws during emergency responses and pursuits. However, the burden for safe driving remains on the police officer. While the exact language

It is extremely common for a fleeing motorist to turn in early, brake late, and simply run out of room as he exits the corner. The Jaguar has ended up three lanes over and is still understeering hard. Don't follow his line and make the same mistake.

varies from state to state, the law places two absolute requirements on the traffic officer during enforcement driving. One, the officer must drive with due regard for the safety of all persons using the highway. Two, the police vehicle gains the right-of-way only when using both emergency lights and siren.

The use of adequate visual and audible warning devices, such as flashing lights and siren, is both a statutory mandate for most pursuit situations and also assures as much as possible that other vehicles and pedestrians are alerted to approaching emergency vehicles.

Overconfidence on the emergency lights and siren to do their job of warning is a real problem. Many drivers are visually distracted or drive with their windows up or radios playing and are not aware of approaching emergency vehicles.

Most departments forbid unmarked vehicles without emergency lights and siren from making high-speed emergency runs or engaging in pursuits. If a particular emergency requires a "silent run," with no siren and lights, the officers must adjust their driving style and speed accordingly. Remember: The emergency lights and siren only requests the right-of-way. Other motorists must grant it.

During emergency driving, keep in mind that the high-pitched sound of a siren is very directional. It travels in a straight line and will bounce off of solid objects such as a car trunk. A siren is more audible where there are buildings and parked cars for the sound to reflect off of than in sparsely populated or open areas. Remember to fluctuate the pitch of the siren from mid to upper range if it is manually operated. A change in pitch will assure audibility for persons who only hear certain tones. Many modern cars are quite soundproof and equipped with stereos and air conditioning systems. Don't assume that other drivers hear you, as you are probably more affected by the sound of the siren than is traffic around you.

The police officer is safer in relying on visual recognition (lights) of his emergency run than on audible (siren) contact. Remember that high beams may be so bright that the motorist in front of you may not be able to see your emergency lights. This is true of the overhead lightbar, and especially true of grille lights, dash lights, and spotlights. Traffic will just consider you another rude driver and may stubbornly resist pulling out of your way for just that reason. Use high beams for visibility at night but use low beams as you overtake traffic, even if it means you are technically over-driving your headlights.

Following Distance

The lead pursuit car should be four seconds behind the violator vehicle. A common error made during a pursuit is being too close to the fleeing vehicle. This in turn causes other errors. A four-second gap allows the lead pursuit car better visibility of the whole situation. It helps to widen his tunnel vision on the violator. More of what is going on will be inside the police officer's restricted field of view. Too close and all the officer will see are the taillights of the fleeing car. Too close also

Once the helicopter arrives at the scene, the pursuing units need to back off and let the air unit run the pursuit. If the police cars back off, the fleeing driver will pay more attention to his driving. *Rick Scuteri*

makes the officer vulnerable to gunfire from the fleeing vehicle.

A large gap will allow the lead pursuit car to drive the correct "line" through corners. The violator will almost certainly brake too late and turn in to the corner too soon. This means he will almost certainly run outside his lane when exiting the turn and, in fact, may run out of road altogether at the exit. If the officer is too close to the violator, he will be sucked in behind the driver and follow the same dangerously wrong line.

Of course, the closer the officer is to the fleeing car, the more likely he will run over whatever the violator runs over. This may not necessarily be tire deflating devices. It may be glass or other debris caused by side swipes or other small collisions the fleeing car has with other obstacles.

Following too closely may also cause the officer to run into the fleeing car when it stops suddenly. This is exactly what happened in the events leading up to the landmark Supreme Court case, *County of Sacramento, California, v. Lewis*. In that case, the cruiser was five car lengths behind a motorcycle at speeds that reached 100 miles per hour.

As speeds increase, the patrol car should increase the gap between himself and the violator. A gap of one-eighth to one-quarter of a mile may be appropriate for high-speed pursuits where it is easy to keep the violator in view. Don't get too close to the fleeing vehicle, even if you can. Leave a four-second interval between your vehicle and the one you are chasing.

When you initiate the pursuit, pull in close behind the violator before activating the emergency lights. Turning on the light gear from a long distance away will just encourage the violator to flee, with the big head start you have given him. Instead, overtake the violator, obtain license plate number and occupant information, then hit the emergency lights. By activating the lights at a close distance behind the violator, the driver will be less likely to be confused who it is you want to pull over.

At some point during the attempted vehicle stop, the situation will change "from" a slow response by the driver to your emergency lights or inattention on the driver's

Most police departments do not want their motorcycle cops involved in high-speed pursuits. The motorcycle has less conspicuous warning signals and offers the police officer very little cover or protection. *Rick Scuteri*

part "to" a failure or refusal to stop, which is resisting law enforcement or a pursuit. Once the officer decides the motorist is not going to pull over, even if the motorist does not speed up and try to flee, the officer must notify the dispatcher of location, direction of travel, estimated speed, description of vehicle and occupants, and what action caused the pursuit.

Once you have hit the lights, back off to the proper four-second gap. This is not a four-car-length gap, but a four-second gap. At 60 miles per hour, a four-second gap is about 100 yards. At 100 miles per hour, a four-second gap is nearly 200 yards. This is not a race. You do not have to pass. This is not a game of tag. You do not have to touch the fleeing car. All you have to do is keep him in sight. The officer needs to follow the violator, not catch him.

Allow more time and distance if road, weather, or traffic conditions are unfavorable. You don't want to rear-end a fleeing suspect if he suddenly stops or crashes, nor do you want to speed past him and into a position of tactical disadvantage if he stops suddenly.

The large gap between the fleeing car and the police car will give the officer plenty

Adrenaline and Pursuits

At approximately 8:30 P.M., Deputy Mel Wright learned from a general radio broadcast that the Greenwood Police were in pursuit of a stolen Ford Mustang now heading from Greenwood into Marion County, going north on Meridian Street (U.S. 31). Deputy Wright was the district patrol officer for that section of his county, so he decided to wait at Meridian and Banta Road to see what developed.

Wright observed the 5.0-liter Mustang, heading north on Meridian with its lights off. Wright fell in immediately behind the speeding Mustang, and they both accelerated west on Banta to Bluff Road, then north on Bluff to Hanna Avenue, turned right on Hanna, and roared east to Meridian again. The stolen Mustang turned north on Meridian and accelerated ahead briefly. Although the Mustang operator was able to make brief gains during turns, Deputy Wright's interceptor engine in his Chevrolet Caprice allowed him to quickly regain the distance.

At this point, Marion County Sheriff's Department (MCSD) Sergeant Mike Himmel fell in behind Deputy Wright and, pursuant to MCSD policy as the secondary pursuit car, began to "call" the chase for the listening radio control dispatcher who, in turn, re-broadcasted the details of the chase to other area police units. While Himmel was himself no slouch at high-speed pursuits, he was the relief sergeant for that section of the county and not readily familiar with the streets.

The careening Mustang went north on Meridian to Troy Avenue, turned right, and sped east to Madison Avenue. Wright listened as Himmel struggled to broadcast accurate information about the location and direction of the pursuit and silently worried that Himmel's lack of knowledge of the streets would leave responding officers confused and ultimately unable to assist in an apprehension. He resisted being distracted by the thought.

Upon reaching Madison, the Mustang made a screeching right turn and headed south in a cloud of burning tires and roadside dust. A short distance later, the driver of the stolen Mustang took the Y-fork off of Madison and turned onto Meridian (U.S. 31) again and fled toward the I-465 on-ramps. As he urged his cruiser to again close up on the fleeing Mustang, Deputy Wright heard responding officers report that they had set up a roadblock to deny the Mustang further access to southbound U.S. 31 and the interstate ramps.

To Mel's dismay, however, the driver of the stolen vehicle simply slowed and drove over the 6-inch concrete median and continued south on U.S. 31. Wright followed suit, grimacing slightly as his patrol car scraped over the concrete barrier. At this point, Himmel terminated his involvement in the chase and chose to work his way past the roadblock officers.

Wright pursued the Mustang south a short distance in the northbound lane, where they both jumped the concrete median again and kept going south on U.S. 31 in the southbound lane. Wright was again calling his own pursuit and realized that the driver of the stolen Mustang was pouring on the gas as the patrol car's speedometer rolled up over 100 miles per hour. "He's heading home," Wright thought to himself as he noted that they would be back across the county line into Greenwood in a few seconds. This seems to be a typical move on the part of a violator during a prolonged chase in an urban area.

The bad guy gets tired of running maneuvers back into his home territory and then ditches the car and tries to flee on foot. Wright marveled at the stupidity of the Mustang's driver that he would choose to flee right back into the teeth of alerted and angry responding officers and marveled again at the competence of the female dispatcher, as she smoothly coordinated the response of numerous city, county, and state officers. These officers managed to block off cross-traffic at the intersections along U.S. 31 as the Mustang roared past, thus protecting innocent people from injury.

Deputy Wright allowed himself a tight grin as the speed of the pursuit topped over 120 miles per hour, grateful that his brother officers had blocked off the side streets. The Mustang slowed and swerved slightly to miss an Indianapolis Police cruiser with a smoking, blown engine in the middle of U.S. 31 and Epler Avenue. The pursuit again resumed speeds over 100 miles per hour and crossed into Johnson County (Greenwood).

The chase proceeded into Greenwood along the still-divided highway through a heavily commercialized mall area and from there into a less-congested rural area. As the Mustang and police Caprice approached a long, sweeping curve southbound on U.S. 31, Wright was astonished to see Johnson County officers as well as various suburban and state officers coming three-abreast, in a flurry of red-and-blue lights, northbound on U.S. 31 in BOTH the northbound and southbound lanes of the highway. The Mustang slowed slightly and tried to reverse direction, but spun out of control in the grass median.

Wright leveled his service pistol at the Mustang's driver and ordered him out of the car and face-down onto the grass. The scene was filled with the surreal flashing of pursuit lights and a crescendo of sirens. After the suspect was cuffed, Himmel pointed out to his men that the arrest belonged to Greenwood, and it was time for all Marion County officers to secure from the detail and get back to their county. Upon returning to their side of the county line, Himmel got everyone together at a Toys 'R' Us lot and began debriefing all who were involved. Wright got out of his car and, due to adrenaline after-burn, wasn't able to stand up. His legs were fine until the pursuit was over and it was time to go home, then they turned to rubber. Wright sat down on a curb, amazed that his legs wouldn't obey him, and sheepishly endured the back-thumping congratulations of his sergeant and fellow officers. A most memorable 21-minute chase.

—Deputy Melvin Wright
Marion County, Indiana,
Sheriff's Department.
Secondary Pursuit and Communication

of time to react to the fleeing driver. It will also give the officer time to decide if he wants to follow the exact path of the driver or a slightly more conservative "line" through the corner. This large gap also helps the officer to get a better view of the bigger picture. The officer is psychologically less involved in the pursuit and able to make better decisions if he is 15 car lengths behind the violator, as opposed to 15 feet behind him.

Where to Look

During the pursuit, the officer should concentrate on one of two places, depending on his distance behind the violator. The natural tendency is to focus on the taillights of the fleeing vehicle. This is the worst thing the officer can do. It will cause him to follow the same path as the fleeing driver and make the same mistakes as the fleeing driver. It means the officer will wait too long to brake for the corners and turn into the corners too soon. It forces the officer to "react" to the violator rather than to "act" independently, and drivethe best way. When the officer reacts, he loses the smoothness in acceleration, braking, and cornering. Choppy driving at high speeds leads to a loss of control. Instead of focusing on the taillights of the fleeing vehicle, the officer should concentrate on either the roadway ahead of his own vehicle or the roadway ahead of the fleeing vehicle.

If the patrol car is well back from the fleeing vehicle where it should be, a sizable danger zone will exist between the patrol car and the violator. In this case, the officer should focus on what is happening on the roadway and at intersections in the zone between the patrol car and the fleeing car.

If the patrol car is close to the fleeing vehicle, and typically this is the case in urban pursuits, the officer should focus ahead of the fleeing vehicle. This will be hard to do because the tendency is to focus on the fleeing car. Instead, he should concentrate on what is 10 to 20 car lengths in front of the violator. This will allow him to see a threat about the same time the fleeing driver sees it. This may allow the officer enough reaction time to avoid colliding into the fleeing vehicle as he brakes for, or collides with, the obstacle.

The second and third pursuit cars should likewise be well back from the primary pursuit car. We have all seen the aerial footage of pursuits in progress. The fleeing vehicle has 15 police cars on its tail forming a giant snake, weaving at high speeds through city streets or freeways. This is the making for a dangerous 16-car pile-up. The number varies by policy, but many departments forbid more than three cruisers in a police pursuit, the primary car and two secondary cars.

The secondary cars should handle all of the communications of the pursuit. Where the cars are, which direction they are headed, traffic violations or collisions that occur during the pursuit, and changing conditions of the traffic.

Communication during a pursuit is a vital tool. The pursuing officer and dispatcher have an obligation to ensure that complete and accurate information is transmitted to all officers involved. Radio discipline should be maintained to provide clear air time in order for officers directly involved to communicate. Unrelated radio traffic should be kept to a minimum, unless an urgent need exists.

Officers in the vicinity from all affected departments should be notified of the pursuit by the appropriate individuals. Other officers should not become involved unless specifically requested to do so.

When conversation is necessary between departments, plain English should be used in place of radio signals to reduce misunderstanding. Supervisors involved in pursuit situations, unless they are the primary pursuing officer, should assume a backup position. The supervisor's role should be to direct and control the pursuit through communications.

As a rule, accidents happen at intersections and on curves, not on straight, flat roads. The time to use the radio is on a straight road, when steering skills are not needed. It is extremely easy to get the microphone cord wrapped up in the steering wheel when turning. In fact, it is almost impossible to prevent this!

Likewise, if the officer has a choice, the radio should be used on a flat road rather than hilly roads, when stopped rather than when moving, and while pacing rather than while overtaking. In fact, the ideal situation is for the second or third pursuit car to take over as much radio communication as possible. The driver of the lead pursuit car is under incredible stress and the most susceptible to the physiological changes associated with pursuit driving. Allowing another officer to handle pursuit communications allows the lead driver to concentrate on the safety of the pursuit. He should only communicate the things seen from his perspective. Let someone else tell dispatch the violator has turned north on Highway 41 from Highway 352.

If you have a partner, the partner should conduct all of the radio traffic. He should state the present location, direction of travel, and an increasingly complete description of the fleeing vehicle as it becomes available. The pursuit may start with a description like a "late-model maroon sedan," then a "Chevrolet Impala SS" then "Indiana plates," then "License Number 4B-1385." Each piece of information helps. Limited information which comes sooner is much more helpful than detailed information which comes later. The officer should constantly update other units when more information is available.

The partner should watch the right side of the road and the intersection while the driver should scan the left side. Constant communication between the two officers is essential.

If you are a solo unit (without a partner) and the lead car in a pursuit, you have to do it all until additional units join the pursuit. At that time, the lead car takes the responsibility for the pursuit, but the second police unit picks up responsibility for all routine communication.

Terminating the Pursuit

A supervisor or any primary pursuing officer should never hesitate to order the termination of a pursuit if conditions warrant. In some pursuit situations, the best decision is to abandon the chase, especially if heavy traffic, highly congested areas, or erratic driving, which endangers others, is involved. By terminating the chase, the fleeing driver has an opportunity to slow down and possibly abandon the vehicle.

The fleeing driver is in a much more powerful car, is not making driving errors, is driving the right line, and shows no sign of giving up. The officer must ask himself, are the risks of continuing the pursuit getting too high? If so, call it off.

Again, motor vehicle pursuit is justified only when the necessity of immediate apprehension clearly outweighs the level of danger created by the pursuit. From a liability standpoint, it does not matter whether an officer is pursuing a known ax murderer or someone who ran a red light. The officer cannot disregard public safety concerns under any circumstances. If he does, even in good faith to capture the subject, and an accident occurs, he risks a judgment of "willful or wanton" misconduct. This will make the officer and his department fully liable, regardless of the officer's intentions.

It is not cowardice or bad judgment to discontinue any pursuits when, the hazards expose the officer and the public to unwarranted risk, especially when the violation is not serious. A pursuit can become mentally consuming. It is easy to become personally caught up in the heat of the chase when the adrenaline starts flowing. Catching the violator becomes a matter of pride. Your vision tunnels in on the violator and excludes the traffic hazards around you. It takes a great deal of restraint and maturity to discontinue a pursuit when the hazards posed to innocent bystanders become too high. An officer would not be reprimanded for terminating a pursuit. However, disciplinary action is probable for officers exercising poor judgment in continuing a pursuit.

Police officers are required by statute to use due care for the safety of others when disobeying traffic laws, such as operating a vehicle on the wrong side of the road, passing on the right, going the wrong way on a one-way street, passing in a "no passing" zone, or proceeding against a traffic signal. These dangerous and high-risk driving maneuvers must be done cautiously. Police are generally held liable for any resulting accidents.

The decision to continue a pursuit in a reckless manner can create liability. A pursuit should be terminated when the hazards of continuing the pursuit outweigh the benefits and purpose for the pursuit. This can be a tough and subjective decision. In hindsight, a pursuit that ends in an injury to the officer or a third party should probably have been terminated. This means 5 to 10 percent of the pursuits we have had should have been called off.

If it is reasonable to conclude that the fleeing motorist will not voluntarily stop and that there is no realistic way of stopping him without recklessly endangering others, the pursuit should be terminated. As the likelihood of apprehension becomes low, the risks of pursuit become greater than the government's interest in pursuing.

Dangerous pursuits should also be terminated when the fleeing suspect has been identified and there is no continuing need for immediate apprehension. Some officers may be reluctant to terminate a pursuit out of fear that fellow officers will view the voluntary termination as an act of cowardice or timidity. Ultimately, do the risks of the pursuit still justify the continued pursuit? What is the likelihood the driver will be apprehended? As the probability of actually taking the driver into custody decreases, the risks of the continued pursuit clearly increase.

10
Rolling and Stationary Roadblocks

Three common techniques are used to passively stop a fleeing motorist and put an end to the dangerous pursuit. These are rolling roadblocks, stationary roadblocks, and the use of tire deflating spikes like the "stop sick."

It is much easier to describe how to do a rolling roadblock than to actually do it. In fact, according to the most savvy, experienced patrol officers and road deputies, the technique is effective about only half the time. However, when it is effective, it is a way to force the end of a pursuit with minimal damage and low risk of injury. That fact alone makes it worth a try a couple of times before more forceful and aggressive options are used.

The technique involves either three or four squad cars. They all overtake and surround the violator car, box it in on three or four sides, and then all slow down at once. This is much, much harder to do than television would lead you to believe.

First, it requires a pursuit long enough to get that number of cruisers involved. Most pursuits are over in three minutes. One extra cruiser is likely during a pursuit, but two or three extra ones all at the right place and at the right time is much less likely. Second, it requires a coordinated and combined effort with extraordinary communications between officers. Any hole formed in the box pattern by a lack of communication will allow the violator to escape.

With a three-car rolling roadblock, the violator is boxed-in on three sides. As soon as everyone is in position, the lead car slows down. Others follow his lead.

Third, it means that all of the cruisers must be able to overtake the violator, almost at will, and that none of them will be closed off or shut out of their driving lanes by the surrounding traffic.

Here is how a rolling roadblock is supposed to work. One cruiser gets in front of the violator and clears the path. This cruiser could have started off in front of the violator, or simply overtakes him. Another cruiser comes from behind the violator. Two cruisers pull alongside, one on either side. With the violator effectively boxed in, all the cruisers slow down at the same time and at the same deceleration rate.

Expect the violator to resist. He may bash side to side, ram the cruiser ahead of him or brake hard causing the cruiser behind him to rear-end the violator. The violator has not resisted arrest up to this point, simply to give up now. Each officer in the rolling roadblock must expect this. Each officer must also know that it is easy to maintain control of his own car when he gets hit, either side to side or front to rear.

Maintaining control of the police car is not the issue. The problem is getting bounced out of position and allowing a hole in the box for the violator to squeeze out. In fact, one may take a number of attempts to do the rolling roadblock until one finally works. It is much easier to pull alongside, in front, of and behind a violator fleeing down the interstate than it is to slow the whole train down once everyone is in position. Yet, that is exactly what needs to be done. Even with a less aggressive, fleeing driver this is hard to do, but it is very easy to practice. Simply take four squad cars out to a restricted-access, four-lane highway. Have three cars close in on the fourth, and have everybody slow down to a stop. Everyone should have their lights and siren on. The squad car playing the violator should turn its police radio to a different frequency than the others.

The rolling roadblock is a challenge, even with a somewhat willing violator. Basically, once everyone is in position, the LEAD cruiser slows down, and all the other officers must simply react to his action or follow his lead. The ideal communications

The three-car rolling roadblock as seen from the driver's seat in the rear car. It works the best when the violator does not have a shoulder that is easy to drive on.

would be from each of the squad cars when each gets in position, then from the lead car when he is ready to start the slow down.

Yes, this technique has risks. The biggest risk is the close proximity to the violator. If the violator produces a firearm, or is known to have a firearm, this technique should be reconsidered.

Another big risk to success is other traffic, not involved with the pursuit. This traffic makes it difficult to get into position without leaving a hole. If the violator has run this hard, this far, evaded capture, and resisted law enforcement this long, you can bet he will squeeze out any hole he can find or make.

Once at a stop, the officers can deploy and place the subject in custody. One problem to be aware of: If a fourth car is used to prevent the violator from exiting out the shoulder, the driver's door on this car will not be able to be opened. This officer must exit from the right side of his car. He, more than anyone else, is under risk from the violator or, especially, passengers in the violator vehicle, and must exit quickly.

Stationary Roadblocks

As one of the last resorts, in cases where the use of lethal force would be justified to prevent serious bodily injury or the death of any person, a stationary roadblock should be considered. Stationary police roadblocks changed forever in the wake of the 1989 Supreme Court decision in *Brower v. County of Inyo, California*. In this case, an 18-wheel tractor trailer was pulled across the road, on the blind side of a curve. This was judged to be an unreasonable seizure, using excessive force.

A roadblock is considered by the courts as a legal seizure. The level of force used must be as reasonable, necessary, and as justified as any other Fourth Amendment seizure. This means the roadblock may slow the violator but not forcibly and unreasonably block him. The use of two bulldozers with blades dropped in the driving lanes, as in the movie, *Vanishing Point*, is out.

The Rolling Roadblock

In January 1995, the Crisp County Sheriff's Office was advised by a Georgia State Patrol dispatcher that a chase was in process northbound on Interstate 75. Crisp County is midway between the Florida state line and Atlanta in south Georgia. I-75 is a major northbound route for drugs from Florida.

Deputies learned that the chase had originated in Cook County, Georgia, 75 miles south of Crisp County, near the Florida state line. The suspect vehicle was a red 1986 5.0-liter Ford Mustang with Florida plates, which traveled at times in excess of 100 miles per hour. The pursuit had been going on for about 40 minutes. The Cook County deputy who initiated pursuit was still involved. The Georgia State Patrol and other sheriff's deputies had joined the pursuit.

Crisp County Sheriff Donnie Haralson made the decision to use stop sticks to slow or stop the pursuit. Six miles inside the county limits, stop sticks were deployed on the interstate and the violator ran over the stop sticks. The tire deflation device was a success, in that the front tires were punctured, and his speeds were reduced to 60 miles per hour. As the tires tore off the rims, speeds were further reduced to 45 miles per hour.

After the stop sticks took out the front tires, the driver continued to attempt to elude the Georgia law enforcement. It became obvious the driver had no intention of stopping. Within minutes, the pursuit would be out of Crisp County and into Dooly County, where construction was under way on I-75. Crisp County authorities took advantage of the lower pursuit speeds and authorized a rolling roadblock to stop the Mustang before it endangered the road construction site just outside their county.

Crisp County deputies and other officers blocked the entrance and exits to the interstate while other units prepared for the rolling roadblock. A Crisp County patrol supervisor passed the suspect vehicle and took a position in front of the violator. Another deputy moved to the right side with officers of other jurisdictions behind the front officer falling in behind the violator. During construction, a deep drop off had been formed in the median, to the left of the violator.

The deputies started to slow down. With no where to go, the violator reduced his speed. The Crisp County patrol supervisor was tapped from the back by the violator a few times, while it is unclear whether this was unintentional or on purpose. However, Crisp County deputies are trained to expect this response during a rolling roadblock. At one point, the front bumper of the Mustang remained in contact with the rear bumper of the front patrol unit. The patrol supervisor continued to apply the brakes and slow down unit the violator came to a stop.

Overtaking the suspect and positioning the patrol cars can consume both a lot of time and a lot of road. The violator was finally forced to a stop by Crisp County deputies 11 miles after running over the stop sticks, just as the cars entered Dooly County. The violator was taken into custody without further incident. No injuries resulted. No damage was done to the Mustang except for the deflated tires and ruined rims. No damage resulted to any of the patrol units with one exception. Two of the chase units suffered flat tires, not realizing how effective, and how unbiased, stop sticks are! With interagency cooperation, well-trained deputies, and informed police supervision, the rolling roadblock can be successful in stopping pursuits.

—*Colonel Billy Hancock*
Crisp County, Georgia, Sheriff's Office

The four-car rolling roadblock boxes the violator in on all four sides. This method is effective about half the time and is not without risks.

The ideal roadblock is a series of police cars arranged in a maze that forces the violator to go slower and slower as he weaves through the cars and finally to a stop. Set up the roadblock in such a manner as to leave an open path through the restricted area. This path should be designed so that it would be necessary to slow down before it is necessary to stop, or that it is possible to proceed through the roadblock but at very low speeds. Stop sticks should be used both before and again during a stationary roadblock.

Construction barricades are ideal but seldom available. Unoccupied police vehicles with emergency lights in operation may be used. The use of city, county, or state highway department vehicles is also an option, again with their amber or strobe warning lights activated.

Stationary roadblocks should only be set up with the authorization of a supervisor. Roadblocks should be authorized only by the supervisor from the department who initiated the pursuit or a supervisor from another department who has been given control of the pursuit by the initiating department.

To avoid creating an unnecessary hazard to pursuing officers and innocent persons, the barricade should be located in an area that provides a safe stopping distance for oncoming traffic. Under no circumstances should a roadblock consist of occupied or privately owned vehicles, and this includes semi trucks. All efforts should be made to remove private vehicles from the path of the pursuit.

Special care is required when using roadblocks to ensure that innocent persons are not placed in a position of danger and that the fleeing motorist is afforded a reasonable opportunity to stop safely. To reduce the risk of liability, it is recommended that roadblocks be placed in a highly visible area to give approaching drivers ample time to stop. Motorists can be warned of the roadblock by appropriately placed lights and flares. Give the violator an opportunity to stop by placing a stationary police vehicle alongside the road with emergency lights activated and an officer in a safe location directing the suspect to stop.

With a lot of interagency cooperation and a controllable interstate system, the rolling roadblock is effective about half the time. Failing that, and unless lethal force becomes justified, the best tactic is often to block off civilian traffic and ride out the pursuit until the violator blows an engine, runs out of gas, or attempts to exit the interstate.

Tire Deflating Devices
In the early 1990s, tire puncturing devices became the main response to pursuit situations by most police departments. The Arizona Highway Patrol was one of the pioneers in the use of tire deflating devices.

A four-car rolling roadblock as seen from the rear police car. Expect the violator to bump the police cars out of position to create an escape route.

These have been used in one form or another for decades and recently perfected by Stop Stick, Inc.

Stop sticks are generally deployed in sets of three. They can be quickly tossed randomly into the driving lane, placed one at a time on the road, snapped together in one long unit, or inserted into a long sleeve. The original stop stick is designed to be used at speeds over 25 miles per hour and on traditional road surfaces. Since then, other versions have been released. Some are intended for lower speeds and parked cars, in an attempt to stop pursuits before they start. Other versions are designed for off-road and nontraditional road surfaces. Still others have been designed specifically for the heavy-duty tires used on buses and semi trucks.

Stop Sticks and Choppers

Deputy Dave Oberholtzer with the Marion County, Indiana, Sheriff' Department had stopped by an Indianapolis area IHOP to get a cup of coffee. As he walked out of the restaurant at Lafayette Road and 16th Street, he observed a motorist hit another car and take off. The deputy tossed his fresh cup of coffee and ran to his 1998 Ford Crown Victoria.

The pursuit was on. It was a cold and wet October night just after midnight. The streets were wet and slippery. Oberholtzer radioed in his location and the fact that he was in pursuit of a green Monte Carlo. The plate could not be read. He knew a partial vehicle description at a sooner time was better than a detailed description later.

One minute into the pursuit, as the 1977 Monte Carlo sped down 16th Street, the deputy radioed in that speeds had reached 85 miles per hour and advised a partial description of the driver. Two minutes into the pursuit, an Indianapolis Police helicopter joined in. This particular chopper had both a video camera and an infrared camera. By this time, Oberholtzer was able to radio a partial plate number.

While the driver nearly struck a few cars when blowing through stop signs, most of the time the driver slowed for intersections and to take corners. The infrared camera picked up the heated wet pavement from the Monte Carlo wheelspin but for the most part, the fleeing driver kept control. After the initial hit and run, the fleeing driver did not strike any other vehicles.

As the helicopter arrived, the deputy asked the pilot to "call" the pursuit. This is standard practice. However, in this case, the chopper was too close to the Indianapolis International Airport. In airport air space, the use of police radio traffic is restricted.

Three minutes into the pursuit, a state police excise officer joined the pursuit in an unmarked Taurus. Oberholtzer asked the officer to "call" the pursuit but got no response. The deputy was too busy with the pursuit to continue with the request. The Monte Carlo continued to race down city streets, making sudden turns in an attempt to lose the deputy. By four minutes, rookie Marion County Sheriff's dispatcher Mark Spitz switched all radio traffic not involved in the pursuit to WS1, another countywide channel.

The pursuit remained on the same frequency. At this time, Oberholtzer radioed that the subject was slowing down and speeding up, looking for a place to bail out. Also at about four minutes into the pursuit, the driver of the Monte Carlo made his first driving error. He spun out on the wet road right in front of the deputy while turning a right-

The stationary roadblock is one of the last resort options. The Supreme Court has judged this kind of roadblock to be a seizure. Some kinds of fully blocked, no-way-out roadblocks are "unreasonable" uses of force.

hand corner. Oberholtzer had maintained enough of a gap to let the Monte Carlo slide sideways to a stop. While the car promptly took off again, the error produced a bonus. The driver was lit up by the squad car headlights. This allowed the deputy to radio a full and complete description of the driver and a full license plate number. At the five-minute mark, a sheriff's department canine unit joined the pursuit. Other MCSD units announced they were ready to deploy the stop sticks. This was tough to do simply because the Monte Carlo changed direction of travel too often to be predictable. In this case, however, they found a good spot and warned pursuing units to back off. At the six-minute mark came the disappointing radio traffic: The Monte Carlo missed both sticks. After the stop sticks were cleared, the K-9 officer and the deputy swapped places. The K-9 officer became the primary pursuit car and Oberholtzer called the pursuit as the secondary car. At seven minutes into the pursuit, a second attempt was made to use stop sticks, but the officer could not get them thrown in time.

By the nine-minute mark, a number of city, county, and state units had joined the pursuit. While the K-9 officer and Oberholtzer were maintaining their proper gap, behind them was a giant "moving Christmas tree." The Indianapolis Police Department (IPD) chopper broke into radio traffic to advise all cars except the primary and secondary units to back off. They did.

After 10 minutes of switch-backs, stop-and-go corners, wheel-spinning acceleration, and hard driving, Oberholtzer radioed that the subject had lost it, and had stacked the vehicle. The driver accelerated too hard making a corner, only to find a parked van partially blocking the road. He spun the car almost all the way around.

The driver exited the car and started to run but his pants were too baggy! He ended up tripping over his own feet, just as Rin Tin Tin overtook him. The MCSD Rottweiler got a number of bites in on him just as an IPD German Shepherd rushed up on him. Officers pulled the dogs away and incredibly the subject started to run again. Not this time. He was cuffed and stuffed.

This pursuit had it all . . . stop sticks, helicopters, back-up units, good communications, proper pursuit gaps, interagency cooperation, canine bites, safe conclusion, apprehended driver and, as a bonus, crack cocaine on the driver. It's a model for "things done right" during a pursuit. The final advice from Oberholtzer, a veteran of 2,000 search and rescue missions with the U.S. Coast Guard in the Great Northwest, is this: Stop and think. Take time to take in what is around you. This helps you fight tunnel vision. Stay as calm as possible.

—Deputy Dave Oberholtzer
Marion County, Indiana, Sheriffs Dept.

The best stationary roadblock is a maze of police cars, all with emergency lights operating, and all unoccupied. The police cars are arranged in a way that forces the fleeing driver first to slow down and then to weave back and forth until he finally stops.

One of the best ways to stop a dangerous pursuit is through the use of tire deflating devices like the stop stick. The stop stick uses hollow quills with steel penetrator tips to progressively deflate a tire in 5 to 10 seconds. It is critical to warn pursuing units where stop sticks will be deployed!

The stop stick has gained acceptance in all 50 states for a number of reasons. Unlike other tire deflation systems, the stop stick has no moving parts, no exposed spikes, and is effective with any side of the device down. Further, the stop stick is trunk-mounted, can be deployed in less than 10 seconds, and weighs just 4 pounds.

Stop sticks can be deployed in a number of ways, including simply by tossing them into the roadway. The ideal method, demonstrated by this Hoosier deputy sheriff, is to pull a sleeve of stop sticks into the road just as the violator approaches. *Stop Stick, Inc.*

As with any deflation device, the fleeing motorist may see the stop stick, even in a black sleeve, and make evasive moves. The technique is to deploy the stop sticks at the last moment or deploy them in a manner that the motorist cannot evade them. Quick deployment is made possible by pulling the stop stick across the road with a string provided with the device.

Again, as with all such devices, it is extremely important for the deploying officer and the pursuing officer to communicate with one another. Once the deployment site has been selected, all area units should be notified. Pursuing units should back way off to avoid running over the same devices hit by the fleeing motorist. The deploying officer should make an attempt to clear both used and unused stop sticks prior to the arrival of pursuing units.

Since these are all controlled deflation devices, it takes 5 to 10 seconds for the tires to deflate. This is useful information for two reasons: one, the fleeing vehicle will continue unaffected for some distance; two, if the police cruiser happens to run over a stop stick—and it happens—the officer will continue to have steering and braking control long enough to safely slow down from pursuit speeds.

11

Take Outs

The rolling roadblock is considered a passive technique. So are the stationary roadblock and the use of stop sticks. If these fail, the officer has one aggressive and highly effective option to literally force the driver off the road. The technique is called different names by different police agencies. The Fairfax County, Virginia, Sheriff's Department, the first major agency to use it, calls it the Precision Immobilization Technique (PIT).

The California Highway Patrol, the second major agency to teach the procedure, calls it the Pursuit Intervention Technique (also PIT). One out of 12 pursuits, that is 8 percent, involving the California Highway Patrol were terminated by a forcible stop. Other names include physical intervention technique (also PIT), tactical vehicle intervention,

legal intervention, rotate-out or, as known around The Bondurant School, as a "vehicle take out." Regardless of the name, the technique is all the same.

This technique is used to forcibly stop the fleeing vehicle after other means of stopping or pulling the vehicle over have proven to be unsuccessful. Forcible stops are just one part of the overall risk management. It is also designed to be used as a VIP and security escort procedure to prevent a hostage taking. The take out was originally designed as a counterterrorist and executive protection measure. Law enforcement started using the technique in the late 1980s. At The Bondurant School, we also teach this technique as self-defense.

In the right scenario, many agencies have found the take out to be the best of

The Bondurant "take out" works equally well from either side of the car. The officer must move his front bumper forward of the rear bumper on the fleeing car.

The officer has pulled into proper position as seen from the driver's seat. The take out from the right side of the car will rotate the fleeing driver off the right side of the road.

the last resort options. The take out involves the police vehicle coming into physical contact with the fleeing vehicle and rotating the violator out of control. This is typically done at speeds up to 35 miles per hour on straight roads and off ramps.

In the early 1990s, the technique was used only by the California Highway Patrol and the Fairfax County Sheriff's Office. No one else understood the technique. Every one confused it with ramming from the rear, Hollywood-style. Or they understood the technique but prohibited it as being too aggressive or too controversial. In the late-1990s, this technique has gained much wider understanding and acceptance. Once the decision has been made to forcibly stop the vehicle, after stop sticks, after rolling roadblocks, and after stationary roadblocks, this is the technique with the most promise. It has been used successfully from coast to coast and from border to border. Few other forcible techniques work, while this one works extremely well. The Des Moines, Iowa, Police are among the latest to successfully use this technique. It is extremely effective.

Setting Up for a Take Out

In setting up the take out, the officer must pick the location to rotate the violator off the road. He must also select the side of the violator car to push. Specifically, the officer must determine which side of the road he wants the violator to end up and then approach the violator from THAT side of the car.

To rotate the violator to the right side of the roadway and off the shoulder, the officer must push the right side of the violator's car. To rotate the violator to the left side of the roadway and into the center median, the officer must push the left side of the violator's car.

This setup is extremely important. Most officers are accustom to pacing, overtaking, or approaching the violator from the left, or driver's side, of the car. On a divided highway, a takeout from this side will put the violator in the median and possibly across the median into oncoming traffic. On a two-lane road, the technique from the left side generally requires the officer to drive in the oncoming lane. Even if the violator is driving on the right side shoulder, the technique will spin the violator car across the oncoming traffic lane. A take out from the left side of the car works well when overtaking the violator who is exiting or entering a freeway ramp where there is no oncoming lane.

For most cases, the best approach is from the right side. This will push the violator across the shoulder and into the side ditch. In fact, the officer can drive on the much safer shoulder to overtake and approach the violator to start the technique.

Getting in Position

The police officer must first overtake the violator. This is almost never a problem. Then the officer must pull up to the rear quarter panel of the violator vehicle. This is a bit more difficult because proper vehicle positioning is important. The officer must have his front bumper between the rear bumper and the rear tire of the violator vehicle.

The violator will frequently allow the officer to put his car right into this position. After all, the violator has been trained by television to expect the forcible move to be a rear bumper ram or a side bash. As a result, even though the police cruiser, with lights and siren activated, moves into the violator's blind spot, it is not generally deemed as a threatening move. If the violator will not allow the officer to slowly approach to this position, the officer must suddenly accelerate from behind and place his police car in this position. At this point, any action by the violator to cut off the officer will simply result in the technique starting sooner rather than later. Once the front bumper of the cruiser is forward of the rear bumper of the violator car, the stage is set.

The police car has the maximum leverage on the violator car with its front bumper just ahead of the violator's rear bumper. The amount of leverage becomes less and less as the police front bumper moves forward. The center of gravity on a four-door sedan is near the driver's seat. Once the police front bumper moves forward of the "B-pillar," the police car can no longer rotate the violator car around its center of gravity. (The B-pillar is the upright between the two side doors on a four-door and behind the door on a two-door.) Instead, it becomes a side-to-side push that seldom works in favor of the officer.

The squad car comes in soft contact with the fleeing car. Then the officer turns the wheel firmly into the fleeing car and hits the gas.

The cruiser is simply pushing the two rear tire patches sideways. If the officer backs off now, an experienced driver may correct for the oversteer and speed away. Stay on the gas.

The fleeing car will rotate right in front of the police cruiser. By this point, the technique will be over faster than either the officer or the motorist can react.

Executing the Take Out

Once in position, the officer pulls his cruiser into soft contact with the violator vehicle. Once contact is made, the officer immediately turns the wheel firmly into the violator vehicle and squeezes on the throttle.

When pushing the subject from the right, into the right-hand side ditch, the violator vehicle will first rotate off the cruiser's left front bumper/fender and actually cross in front of the cruiser. The cruiser will then bump the violator with its right front fender/bumper. The violator will be off the roadway with the rear end continuing to rotate around. In most cases, with the procedure done at 35 miles per hour, the violator will end up facing backward and well off the road.

Once the process starts, if it is done right, it happens faster than either the violator or

Taking Out an Armed Robber

I grew up in northern Indiana, where dirt track racing is second only to basketball in popularity. I raced stock cars on Friday and Saturday nights throughout the summers. Of course, we all knew how to spin out the race car ahead of us, but never called it a PIT maneuver.

I was on a bank detail in Indianapolis. Every day we would transport important documents in a bank bag from Butler University to a nearby bank. En route to the bank I overheard a dispatch from IPD about an armed robbery in progress at 56th Street and Illinois. I was just one block away.

I pulled the patrol car into the Standard Oil station at that intersection to watch. The next thing I saw was a butcher, complete with bloody apron, running down the street, screaming and waving his meat cleaver, chasing after a red Toyota sedan. I spoke briefly with the out-of-breath butcher who confirmed that the driver of the red Toyota was the armed robber. I gave pursuit, and with my 350-ci Caprice overtook the compact car in a few blocks.

The driver of red Toyota saw my emergency lights, suddenly turned onto the next side street, and took off. He was clearly fleeing. It was winter, with patches of snow and ice on the road. I wanted to stop this pursuit before the fleeing driver hurt someone in the residential area or reached a major intersection.

I had enough power to overtake the Toyota at will, which gave me a lot of control over the situation. I waited until I could find the best spot to force a stop. I saw an intersection coming up and a parked van near the intersection. That was what I was looking for. In the city, we don't have a median or side ditch like the rural areas. The best way to trap a fleeing car is to push him into a parked vehicle.

At about 30 miles per hour, I pulled past his rear bumper, gradually came in contact, and powered into his side. You are not supposed to bash into the side, but come in gradually. As I spun him around, the driver tried to correct for the spin, overcorrected, lost control and smacked into the curb, flattening both front tires. He skidded for a half a block down the sidewalk with parked cars on one side and picket fences on the other. His attempted correction allowed him to miss the parked van that I had targeted. He eventually slid to a stop.

The subject bailed out of the car. A vehicle pursuit turned into a foot pursuit, over one picket fence after another. After a few hurdles, I lost him, but IPD picked him up a couple hours later trying to break into a house. The subject left $60 in cash and his gun in the car.

That was nothing compared to what I left in my car! To give foot pursuit, I stopped the cruiser right in the middle of the street, leaving the car door wide open. On the front seat was the Butler University bank bag. I didn't know exactly what was in the bag, which usually contained documents and checks, but I knew it was important. For just this reason, while chasing the subject on foot, I radioed to responding units to secure my squad car. I later found out the bag contained $100,000 in cash! The department promptly changed its policy, requiring all bank bags to be placed in the trunk during transport.

—Lieutenant John Keiper
Butler University (Indiana) Police

Once the officer is sure the violator car is on its way off the road, he should stand on the brakes. This will transfer weight to the front tires of the cruiser and help the officer control his own car.

officer can react to it, and is over before either driver can correct for it. As soon as the officer sees the technique is working, he should straighten the wheel and continue to accelerate. Continued acceleration will prevent even a well-trained violator from correcting and pulling out of the slide you have put him in. Once a driver realizes what is happening and corrects for it, from that time on he will protect his rear quarter panels and not allow you to get near them.

As soon as the technique is over and the violator has spun off the road, the officer should brake as hard as he can. Now is the time to activate the ABS. If done properly, the cruiser will come to a safe stop, squarely in its driving lane. The violator car will likely be off the road to the officer's right *facing* the cruiser.

The entire procedure is a smooth, quick, and firm quarter turn on the steering wheel followed immediately by acceleration and quickly straightening out the wheel. As quickly as possible, move the steering wheel so the hands, once at 3 and 9, are at 6 and 12, then just as quickly are back to 3 and 9.

Ideal Take Out Speeds

The technique works at nearly any speed, including very low speeds such as 20 miles per hour. The technique also works at much higher speeds, and in fact, can be seen in action from time to time during NASCAR stock car races. However, the recommended speed is 25 to 35 miles per hour. At these speeds, the officer can easily force the violator vehicle off the road and the patrol vehicle is almost unaffected by the process. At these lower speeds, the violator vehicle slides off the roadway and comes to a rest quickly with little risk of rolling over.

At higher speeds, even if the technique is done perfectly correct, it is increasingly difficult to keep the police cruiser under control even with hard braking and rapid steering corrections. At speeds above 35 miles per hour, the chances rise dramatically for the police cruiser to spin off the roadway. At higher speeds, the effects on the violator vehicle also rise dramatically. The chances increase for multiple roll-overs, serious injury, or death to the violator and extensive property damage caused by the violator vehicle. The rolling roadblock is a good option where speeds are just too high for a physical interception.

Other Techniques

Driving technique, not vehicle size, is the key to success. Officers will find that Hollywood-style ramming only works on TV. Ramming the rear bumper or wiping the rear bumper side-to-side with the front bumper of the squad car is not effective in forcing a stop. A drill involving a couple of very hard rear thumps easily proves this. The door-handle-to-door-handle side bashing is not effective either. The police vehicle has to be twice as big as the fleeing vehicle

The front of the squad car may get bounced around a little as the fleeing car rotates around the cruiser. The cruiser will tap the fleeing car just as the car spins off the road.

for this to work. Side bashing is not only unreliable, it also places the officer at risk from gunfire by the violator.

The front-cut-off technique still taught at some police academies does not work either. With this technique, the squad car pulls in front of the violator car and turns into the violator to force him off the road. With just a little resistance, even unintentional resisting, the violator car can actually spin the police squad off the road.

When performed as instructed, the tactic finishes with the violator spun around backward on the shoulder or in the median. Once at rest, the violator can be blocked from escape by other responding vehicles, end up simply stuck in the sand or mud, or be sufficiently intimidated by the rough spin-out to give up the flight.

When performed at urban traffic speeds, the take out easily spins the violator backward and off the road. In training, the violator sustains no injuries whatsoever, and the violator car receives only minor fender damage. The patrol car receives only scratches and sometimes no damage at all. This technique ends with the officer still on the road and puts him at a safe tactical distance. It also gives him the most options on how to proceed.

Many pursuit policies allow officers to take out violator cars, but only under strict guidelines. The offense or action of the driver must warrant the use of deadly force. The officer must consider numerous factors, such as the geographic location, oncoming traffic, and presence of pedestrians. The stop must follow approved tactical felony stop procedures. This is an enforcement tool that can be effective, but its use is also heavily regulated.

This tactic is useful in only a very small window of opportunity for a patrol officer. The take out is taught so that if it has to be done as a last resort, it can be done safely. Each agency that teaches this technique to its traffic officers puts tight controls on when it can be used. The instruction in this technique typically includes a refresher on the strict take out policy. Most of these progressive agencies will not use the take out on a vehicle with hostages or children or one with nonfelony occupants in the vehicle.

The liability of the rotation tactic raises tough questions, but the tactic itself is quite easy. It does not make any difference whether the violator's car is front-wheel drive or rear-wheel drive. Same for the patrol car. Nor does it matter the physical size of either vehicle. Today's mid-size police cars like the Chevrolet Lumina can easily rotate out the biggest Chryslers and Buicks, if the technique is done properly.

This technique is intended to be used as a last resort, when the use of lethal force would otherwise be authorized and justified. In fact, that is how the officer knows when it is the right time to use this technique. If the threat to the general public is high enough for the officer to be justified in actually shooting the driver, the threat is high enough to justify forcibly taking the vehicle out. At lower speeds, unless the violator vehicle strikes another object, the vehicle will likely spin around to a safe enough stop that the officer better prepare himself for a foot pursuit. At higher speeds, the vehicle will likely end up in a very violent one-car collision.

Things can, indeed, go wrong. The officer can lose control of the cruiser. This is most likely to happen at higher engagement speeds. It can also happen if the officer aggressively slams into the violator vehicle. The technique is to make soft contact, and then push, not steer violently into the fleeing vehicle. The other problem is bumper entanglement. Unless the cruiser accelerates hard in an attempt to keep the pivoting and the rotation going rapidly, the two bumpers can lock, depending on bumper design. While this will effectively halt the pursuit, it may also put the officer in a vulnerable position. He may end up way too close to the violator in a tactically compromised position.

The officer has the option to end the technique differently. Taken a step further, the officer can maintain contact with the violator car and can actually pin it against a guard rail or other natural barrier. This is a special response technique in use by a number of federal teams.

Instead of separating from the violator car, the officer can turn into the violator's car and actually push the violator off the road. Ideally, this would end up with the

At this point, the officer will want to point his wheels straight ahead. The technique is a hard quarter-turn of the steering wheel into the fleeing car, then a hard quarter-turn back.

violator car pinned against a barrier on one side with the front end of the cruiser pinning the other side doors closed. Yes, this is an extremely aggressive move. Yes, it puts the officer in very close proximity to the violator. However, it absolutely stops the violator vehicle from reentering the roadway after recovering from the spin.

It also absolutely stops the occupants from fleeing the vehicle. This is the way to stop vehicles that cannot be otherwise stopped or that have been spun out only to regain traction and take off again.

The officer's approach to the violator vehicle is the same. The front bumper of the cruiser goes between the rear bumper and the rear tire of the violator car. The soft contact with the hands at the 3 and 9 position on the wheel is the same. The firm nudge rotating the steering wheel a quarter turn is the same. The differences start immediately after the nudge. Instead of straightening the steering wheel, the officer actually turns the wheel the opposite direction. The violator will cross sideways in front of the cruiser, and then continue to rotate out of the way of the cruiser.

At this point, the officer turns the wheel from a quarter turn one direction to a quarter turn the opposite direction and actually drives his front bumper right into the violator's B-pillar. With his car now in a T-bone vehicle position, the officer continues to accelerate and actually pushes the

Unlike many forcible vehicle techniques, the take out is easy to do and works extremely well. The officer ends up squarely in his own driving lane while the violator ends up off the road and sometimes stuck. Keep the speeds at 35 miles per hour or less for the best results.

violator vehicle sideways off the roadway and into either a berm or guardrail or until both vehicles come to a rest. The violator car, skidding sideways, loses speed rapidly, and acts as a cushion for the cruiser.

This technique does not work well at speeds over 35 miles per hour, because things simply happen too fast for the officer to react to. This technique also requires considerably more training, experience, and practice than the take out technique. Significantly, while the occupants of the violator vehicle will be both disoriented and pinned in the car, the officer will end up just a hood's length away from possibly armed subjects. It is possible his door may be jammed closed. It is possible the air bag may also inflate.

This is a high-risk maneuver. At lower speeds, with an experienced officer, this technique works as intended roughly half the time. For these reasons, this technique has typically been taught only to military special forces and elite federal law enforcement teams. However, as perpetrators increasingly use military-style assault tactics, like the North Hollywood, California, shoot-out, police officers will increasingly use military-style counter-measures. This is one.

Whether or not the officer uses the take out to end a pursuit, he or she should still be aware of both the technique and the countermeasures to prevent it from being used on the police cruiser. This is especially true for officers involved in VIP protection and prisoner transport. Do not fall victim to this technique. Understand that you can be easily taken out by this procedure.

Do not allow a vehicle a clear shot at your rear fenders. Instead, be ready to accelerate to give the threat vehicle only the back of your rear bumper. Acceleration will also place much-needed weight on your rear wheels and give your car more traction and more resistance to being spun out.

If you have been compromised either by a surprise tactic or by the side-to-side bash that happened to impact behind your rear wheel, correct for the rear-wheel skid and accelerate. You need weight on the rear wheels for traction. On a front-wheel drive police car, heavy acceleration is enough to pull the car out of the slide and not enough to cause front-wheel spin due to the weight transferred to the rear.

If you do recover from the first attempt, let that be a lesson. Protect your rear quarters even if it means pulling to the inside of every turn where you would normally, and correctly, hold to the outside longer. Remember, when you do the take out, you do it at speeds around 35 miles per hour. The threat vehicle may attempt this at highway speeds where the results could easily be a roll-over or fatal impact.

Take outs should only be considered to stop a fleeing vehicle as a last resort, and then only in those extreme cases in which the use of force is justified to prevent injury or death to the officer or other persons. The officers must consider the extreme danger to themselves and other users of the highway. Firearms will be used only when the use of deadly force is justified.

Over the past 10 years, the concept of police vehicle intervention has gained nationwide acceptance. Understandably, different variations of the same theme have begun to show up. Some of these variations, however, are risky and ill-advised. One such technique involves a primary and a secondary pursuit car in a high-risk stop. The primary vehicle pulls alongside the violator, then rotates the violator off the road. This primary pursuit car then performs a U-turn, and pulls in front of the violator, blocking his exit to the front. The secondary pursuit car pulls in behind the spun-out violator, blocking his exit to the rear. The officers from the secondary car perform high-risk vehicle stop procedures while officers from the primary car get out of the line of fire.

Pursuits seldom go according to a plan. Everyone gets pumped up and out of position or out of communication. It is likely that one of the violators will exit his car before the officers in the primary car

The California Highway Patrol was one of the first agencies to use the Pursuit Intervention Technique, a.k.a. the take out. Their training cars have an elaborate, ladder-frame, tube-bumper to allow the technique to be repeated over and over without damaging the vehicle.

get out of the way. The officers in the secondary car will tunnel-vision on the violators and may not see the officers behind the violators.

A better plan is to have the primary car stop in the middle of the roadway, next to the spun-out violator. Have the second pursuit car stop behind the violator. Now it is the violator who gets caught in a crossfire. Between the two police cars, the officers can see all four sides of the violator. This will be important if the violator vehicle is a van or other large vehicle. More importantly, no police officers will get hurt if someone has to shoot before everyone gets in position.

This technique must be practiced a few times to learn and then periodically to keep the technique skills sharp. The biggest problem with practicing is that the technique slowly tears up the cars, turning them into refugees from a demolition derby.

At The Bondurant School, we mounted a large V-shaped bumper on an older school car. This allows us to use the take out car over and over again without damage. Police departments can buy wrecking yard cars that still run. Some agencies mount elaborate bumpers around the front of the take out car and around the rear of the violator car.

12
Defeating the Roadblock

One of the more aggressive techniques taught to law enforcement and antiterrorist drivers is the correct way to defeat a stationary roadblock. This technique might be used by a police officer when transporting or escorting a high-profile prisoner. It also might be used by a chauffeur or private security force protecting or escorting a VIP.

The Bondurant School developed the technique for the Executive Protection/Anti-Kidnapping Course. It works easily and every single time. Every Bondurant School student has been able to learn the technique in a matter of hours.

Say you are on a VIP or a prisoner transport detail and someone has aggressively blocked the road in front of you. For the safety or security of your passengers, you make the high-risk decision to ram the roadblock.

The blocked car will move out of the way easily because it is only sitting on two small tire patches on either end of the car. The entire car rests on four tire patches, but the end you are going to hit only has two small tire patches, and the car will spin around easily. Even the impact is little more than just a bump.

Antiroadblock Technique

As you approach the blocking vehicle, reduce your speed to somewhere between 15 and 20 miles per hour. About five car lengths

Some prisoner transport and VIP escort duties call for the police officer to ram a stationary roadblock. Slow down to about 20 miles per hour. About five car-lengths away, accelerate. *Greg Fresquez*

Aim for whichever end of the car you want to rotate out of the way. Aim for the space between the bumper and the wheels on either the front or the rear. *Greg Fresquez*

from the blocking vehicle, accelerate at near full throttle and aim for either the front or the rear quarter panel. Simply rotate the vehicle out of your way and accelerate up to highway speeds to escape the trap.

Very slow speeds work extremely well. At speeds under 15 miles per hour, it becomes a matter or shoving the blocking vehicle out of the way. At higher speeds, the impact of the collision bounces the blocked vehicle out of the way.

It will be knocked completely out of the way with very little damage to your car. The key is to hit the point of least resistance. If the blocking car is at a right angle to your vehicle, hit the rear-end and rotate it the other way. The rear-end is the point of least resistance because the majority of the car's weight is in the front due to the engine. If the blocking vehicle is at an angle, ram the side that is angled away from the ramming vehicle.

The ram is not intended as a high-speed, heavy-impact procedure. Instead, it involves a low-speed impact followed by a shove, or series of shoves, as the blocking vehicle is skidded out of the way.

The police vehicle should be aimed directly for the quarter panel or fender. The center of the hood should strike midway between the blocking vehicle's wheel and bumper. With this point of impact, the police vehicle needs only to push half the weight of the blocking vehicle out of the way. Even on a 4,000-pound full-size car, this means pushing just 2,000 pounds with only the resistance of friction from the two small tires patches.

The police vehicle should NOT strike the blocking vehicle anywhere between the front and rear tires. Specifically, the police vehicle should avoid, if possible, hitting the front or rear doors of the blocking vehicle. Impacts between the wheels, a T-bone impact, means the police vehicle will end pushing the entire weight of the blocking car. It also means the vehicle will remain squarely in front of the police vehicle, and not be rotated out of the way.

We ran the drill at The Bondurant School specifically for photos for this book. Even though the impact vehicle was a 2,890-pound Ford LTD against a 3,470-pound Caprice acting as a blocking vehicle, the Taurus remained perfectly on course after the impact. The LTD also remained squarely in its own traffic lane, even with a high-impact speed.

The technique works well because the incoming vehicle only has to push half the blocking car weight. Only two small tire patches need to be overcome. *Greg Fresquez*

At very low-impact speeds, the ram becomes a series of bumps moving the car out of the way. At higher speeds, the impact of the collision bounces the blocking car out of the way with the first hit. *Greg Fresquez*

The ramming vehicle will probably be driveable after the impact, especially if the impact speed is low. This is a major advantage of keeping the speeds to a minimum. You do not want to push the fan blade into your radiator or crush the front fenders into your front wheels. The blocking vehicle may also be driveable. In fact, be prepared for the rammed vehicle to suffer so little damage that it might be used to pursue you.

Keep Impact Speed Low

Many good reasons exist for using a low-impact speed. First, this is all that is needed! In fact, with enough traction, the impact speed can be zero. From a standing start, the police vehicle can rotate the blocking vehicle out of the way.

Secondly, the higher impacts can have an adverse effect on today's electronically controlled squad cars. The biggest problem is a sensor detecting an impact and shutting off the electric fuel pump. The police vehicle may move the blocking vehicle out of the way but will shortly stall from lack of gasoline and roll to a stop, close to where the trap was originally set. Another reason for keeping the impact speed low is to minimize front end damage to the police vehicle. Low speeds work very well,

while speeds over 25 miles per hour should not be used.

Air Bag Deployment

Another problem is the possible deployment of the air bag. Every police package vehicle since 1992 has had a steering wheel-mounted air bag, which in most makes is designed to deploy as a result of the equivalent of a frontal impact with a stationary object at around 18 miles per hour. When you ram the roadblock, expect the air bag to deploy.

With the officer's face back away from the steering wheel and thumbs clear of the steering wheel, the deployment is a short-term problem. Assuming the car still has a fuel supply, the vehicle can be driven with a deployed air bag. The first few seconds after impact will be pretty exciting though. What you do in the next two seconds will be the difference between no injuries, minor injuries, serious injuries, or even deaths.

Get your hands, wrists, and arms out of the path of the air bag. Using a 3 and 9 hand position, air bag will go right between your hands and the horn button will also go between your hands. The air bag and horn button have enough power to break your arms or your hands if they are struck.

If you have your hands up at 2 and 10 and the air bag goes off, the horn button may injure your arms.

Specifically, get both your thumbs out of the path of the deployment zone. Hold the steering wheel from the outside rim with your palms. Put your head back against the headrest to keep your face as far away as possible from the deploying air bag. The air bag will inflate and deflate faster than you can detect with the eye.

When High Speeds Are Unavoidable

What about the more serious, high-speed collisions? What should you do if an accident is imminent and unavoidable? Don't freeze. You must take action. What you do in the next two seconds could be the difference between minor injuries and death or serious injuries and no injuries at all.

The officer should avoid a head-on collision at all costs. In the event of an impending crash, try to strike an obstacle at a glancing angle. Given the choice, the officer should collide with the right front fender first. Even a collision with the left front fender is preferable to a head-on crash.

When you see that a collision is going to happen, take a deep breath and relax your arm and leg muscles. The deep breath also relaxes your neck and shoulder muscles. Do not push down on the pedals or steering wheel to brace yourself. On a frontal impact, you can break your arms and legs doing that. Cops are always amazed that a drunken driver so frequently escapes serious injury in a serious crash. The reason is the drunk's body is relaxed.

See if you can drive out of it and avoid the collision all together. Say a car is coming across the centerline, headed toward you. A quick lane change or even an aggressive two-lane swerve may avoid the collision. Full ABS activation and a quick half-turn of the wheel are needed. At highway speeds, this maneuver will probably result in your spinning out. However, you will have avoided a front end, head-on collision and the certainty of serious injury and near-death.

When a driver comes left of center, it is a pure gamble on whether you should turn to your left or to your right to avoid him.

He is coming to your right, you turn to your right, he continues to come and the two cars collide. If you swerve to your left, however, you have two problems. First, the driver may suddenly realize he has crossed the center line and pull back in his lane, just as you are pulling into his lane to avoid him. Second, a bigger problem exists, believe it or not, along about now. Swerving left, across the center line now has you facing oncoming traffic. You may have missed the first driver, who has continued to drive off to your right, but you may now collide with traffic in the driving lane behind the original driver. The best bet, and it is only a bet, is to swerve to the

The ramming vehicle easily pushes the blocking vehicle aside, leaving a completely open lane. The ramming vehicle is not tossed off course at all. *Greg Fresquez*

Low-impact speeds work the best for the roadblock ram. Low impact speeds are least likely to set off an air bag in the police car and are the least likely to shut off the electronic fuel pump. *Greg Fresquez*

Chances are the ramming vehicle will be driveable after the ram. Even this Taurus is driveable after executing multitudes of 30-mile-per-hour rams. Lower speeds minimize radiator damage and sheetmetal wrinkling.

right and keep pulling to the right. Go into the shoulder, and off the roadway altogether into the ditch to avoid a head-on collision.

If you are headed for a stationary object like a wall, parked car, or bridge abutment, try to hit the object at an angle. Try to

glance or bounce off the object. If the car is spinning around, try to back into the object at an angle. You won't have the impact that you would if you hit it directly. If you can spin the car around and hit it at the angle at the back, you have a headrest that will help save your neck.

In the event of an impending collision, get your hands, especially thumbs, out of the way of the air bag. Your seat belt should have already been on.

Avoid a head-on collision, no matter what you have to do. The best bet is to drive off the road to your right. Try to hit stationary objects at an angle, rather than head-on. Take a deep breath, let it out, and ride out the collision. *Rick Scuteri*

13
Adverse Driving Conditions

Police cars are driven in all kinds of inclement weather. Police officers do not have a choice of the weather they drive in. When called, they must respond, period. Adverse driving conditions can range from glare ice on the roadway in the middle of dense fog to gravel on the roadway in a corner on a bright sunny day. Adverse driving conditions include "road condition" problems such as ice, snow, slush, water, gravel, sand, or any other foreign material on the roadway. Adverse driving conditions also include "visibility problems" such as dense fog, driving rain, blinding snow (white out), and freezing rain that affects visibility.

Weather conditions such as ice, snow, fog, sleet, rain, wind, heat, humidity, cold, smoke, and hazy conditions may reduce visibility as well as traction. In snow and ice, the edge of the road, lane markings, or even traffic signs may not be visible. The stopping distance on ice and snow increases dramatically with greater speed.

Good Tires at Appropriate Speeds

Driving under adverse conditions is much different than driving under ideal conditions. The two keys to driving under adverse weather conditions are good tires and reduced speed. Follow the basics and slow down. It really is as simple as that. Adverse conditions are simply a call to the return to the basics of driving.

When you drive, sit upright. It is easier to sense and feel the car. It keeps you alert. A lot of times you can sense and feel when you can get yourself in trouble.

Hydroplaning

Suppose it's raining. Don't get yourself in a situation where you are going too fast for the weather conditions. This means slow down. If you drive too fast, you will start to

Dropping a tire off the roadway is common. So are single-car accidents that result from the wrong response in this situation.

Back off the gas. Don't touch the brakes. Get the car settled down.

Don't panic. Just turn the wheel straight. Let the rear tire come down to join the front one. Don't try to jerk the wheel back.

hydroplane, meaning that the tires move on top of the surface of the water rather than on the surface of the road. Hydroplaning greatly affects steering and braking.

The solution to hydroplaning is braking. Slow down before hitting large areas of water. Turn on your windshield wipers before hitting water. Tap your brakes as you exit water to evaporate water from the rotors. It is always a good idea to turn on your headlights any time you use your windshield wipers; in fact, some states require it.

Four factors contribute to hydroplaning. All of these are interrelated. One is water depth. The deeper the water, the more you will hydroplane and the lower the speed that hydroplaning will occur. Before hydroplaning can exist, there must be sufficient water depth of standing or flowing water to submerge tire tread. The second is tread depth. The deeper the tread, the more water the tires can handle before hydroplaning. Tires with a more open tread (like "mud and snow" tires), ones with a wide water-clearing channel (like the Goodyear AquaTread) or

tires with a large number of sipes (tiny cuts in the tread) handle water better than those without these features.

The third factor is tire pressure. Tires with lower tire pressure are easier to hydroplane than those with higher tire pressure. The fourth factor is vehicle speed. The faster you go, the more you are likely to hydroplane. The absolute solution to hydroplaning, once it starts, is to slow down. Vehicle speed is the only factor you have under your control at this point.

The only way you can get out of that situation is ease off the gas. If your police car has ABS brakes, squeeze the brakes on, slowing the car down. You will have traction again. You will not have to slow down much. The difference between hydroplaning and traction is often just one or two miles per hour.

The roads will be more slippery during the first few hours of rain than after it has rained for a day. Remember when you are driving on the first rain that you have got a lot of oil and rubber down on the asphalt and the roads are going to be slippery.

Driving in Snow

When you are driving in snow, you obviously have similar control problems. Slow down. Sense and feel the car. Look where you want to go. Look for other people spinning out of control. The most challenging type of driving is on ice. You want to be smooth. You want to keep it slow.

Pick your spot to drive back up on the roadway. Stay off the brakes. Turn the steering wheel up to a quarter-turn to reenter the road.

Simply turn the wheel and drive right back on to the road. Keep off the gas and brakes.

The best advice for driving on snow or ice is to have snow tires on the vehicle and slow down. Have a shovel, tow rope, and tire chains available. Make sure that the vehicle heater and defrosters are in good working order. When starting from a stop, straighten the front wheels on a snow-covered or slippery surface so the rear-drive wheels don't have to push turned front wheels. When driving through deep snow, shift into a lower gear before entering the snow and attempt to keep the car moving. When stopped or stuck in deep snow or in a snow drift, be aware that carbon monoxide may seep back into the vehicle.

Pay attention to the ambient temperature. Wet roads with ice and freezing rain are the most treacherous of all driving conditions. Bridges and shaded roadway areas freeze first.

If you get into trouble in any of these situations, remember that ABS can save you. Push on the brakes fairly hard, and you will feel the brake pedal pulsate, and the car starting to get under control again. Remember, the tires have to be rotating to give you control. If the wheels are locked up, you have gone from a nice tire footprint down to almost nothing. With no traction, you are just going along for the ride until you hit something.

For all these adverse road conditions, you want to have good tires. That is not always possible, depending on your department. However, when you are in bad

Depending on the condition of the shoulder and the height of the drop-off, you might feel a bump as you get back up on the road.

weather, emphasize to your supervisor the importance of tires with good, deep tread.

When you drive under adverse road conditions, even with good tires, you really learn the limits of your car. You learn to be a lot smoother and more precise.

Off-Pavement Driving

If you are driving off-road, on a gravel or dirt road, on a sandy beach or off-road terrain, you want to get to know your vehicle very well. Test your vehicle control skills. Firmly but gently, apply the brakes. Did the ABS activate? In a non-ABS car, did one of the tires lock up? Was it more slippery than you thought? Lightly and gently, put your vehicle in a bit of a slide. Control it with power, not jumping on the gas. Not a great big slide so you spin it out. Just use your head. Feel what the slide is going to do, so you know how to control it in a given situation.

Remember that in all of these conditions you have less traction than you do on asphalt. Sense and feel the vehicle. Get to know your vehicle well.

If you do have to drive on soft surfaces, like the beach, make sure you don't make abrupt turns at corners. You can dig your front tire right into the sand and roll your vehicle. If you are on off-road terrain, use your eyes and really look at the road. Don't try to go too fast too soon.

If you have an off-road recovery situation where you have really gotten into a big slide and you are starting to go off-road with it, turn the wheel straight and drive it

Once up on the road with full traction again, the car will want to cross lanes into oncoming traffic. Don't forget to correct the wheel.

Don't forget to unwind the wheel! As soon as you get on the road, firmly turn the wheel back a half-turn.

You straightened the wheel when you went off-road, then you turned hard left to reenter, then hard right to correct. Now straighten the wheels for a full recovery.

The two keys to maintaining control under adverse road conditions such as snow and slush are to slow down and have good tires.

When driving on soft surfaces, such as a sandy beach, don't make sharp turns. The front tires could dig in and roll the vehicle. Get a feel for how your vehicle handles under these conditions.

A gravel or dirt road can provide surprisingly little traction! Try the ABS. Try putting the car in a tiny slide to check for traction. Under ideal conditions, a gravel road is more slippery than water-soaked blacktop.

For the most control under all adverse road conditions, be sure your tires have good, deep tread. Asymmetric tread tires, first introduced on the Ford Taurus, are the best choice for police vehicles.

straight off the road. Stay off the gas. Stay off the brakes. Let the car settle down and then come back on the road gently.

To practice this, at low speeds, drop a front wheel off the road on a dirt road. Stay off the gas and brakes. Don't jerk the wheel back. Instead, let the rear-wheel come off the road, too. Let the car stabilize, then gently turn the steering wheel to drive back onto the road.

Don't be in a big hurry to get back on the roadway. That's how you spin it out and roll it. Depending on the height of the drop-off, or the softness of the shoulder, this might take up to a quarter-turn of the wheel to bring the wheels back on the road. Once back on the road, remember to unwind the steering wheel with a quarter-turn of the wheel. The car will want to cross traffic lanes quickly once traction is regained. Unwind the wheel. Uncorrect for the recovery.

Finally, especially under adverse conditions, keep a four-second gap between your car and the car in front of you. Do not make any sudden moves with the steering wheel, brakes, or accelerator. This could cause skids. Slow down in advance of intersections, curves, and downgrades, sooner than you would under normal conditions.

When the car starts to hydroplane, the only solution is to ease off the gas. Frequently the difference between traction and no traction is just a few miles per hour.

14

In-Service Training

Emergency response and pursuit driving are both considered by the courts to be a usual and recurring part of police duty. In 1989, the Supreme Court sharply increased the pressure on police agencies to provide adequate training for all normal and expected police duties. In *Canton, Ohio, v. Harris*, the Court held that inadequate training may serve as a basis for a Title 42, Section 1983, civil rights action. The Court wants to see a written policy, wants the policy uniformly enforced, and wants training specifically geared toward that policy. Failure to do so amounts to what the Court called "deliberate indifference" to victims' constitutional rights. This ruling essentially made driver training mandatory for recruits, veteran officers, and reserves.

Police departments can find a place to practice driving skills, if they would only look. This car is being tossed around on a 3/8-mile stock car oval. A pylon chicane keeps the speeds below 60 miles per hour.

The Hall County, Georgia, Sheriff's Department uses the skid pad at Road Atlanta to hone wet weather skills. The flooded pavement is giving the Mustang driver a chance to correct for oversteer at very low speeds. *Dave Moon*

Pursuit and high-speed driving is more hazardous than most cops will admit. It often catches their driving ability off guard. The fact is that insurance companies pay out more claims related to vehicles than all of the other police-related claims combined, including firearms.

Officers who have graduated from the police academy in the past 10 years probably have had some form of Emergency Vehicle Operations Course (EVOC). EVOC, as necessary as it is, is geared toward low-speed accident avoidance. Many officers have had no training at all in high-speed techniques. They get training in firearms, due to the extreme liability of firearms, but they do not get training in driving, because "everyone knows how to drive."

Formal, in-service driver training for police officers reduces the probability of officer-induced accidents. For example, the Georgia State Patrol experienced a 30 percent reduction in the number of pursuit-related accidents for officers who had received high-speed training. Good drivers are made, not born.

Fast Versus Slow Training

Current police vehicle training is generally divided into two approaches. One is the low-speed, EVOC-style, precision maneuvers course held in small parking lots. This is low-risk training that focuses on the reduced speed capabilities of the car. The

limits of tire adhesion are seldom exceeded. Nearly all officers are exposed to this form of driver training at the academy.

The other approach is the high-speed, pursuit-style, road racing course held on race tracks or air strips. This is high-risk training to which fewer officers are exposed. Loss of control on these courses could result in violent spins. It is difficult for the police instructor, as a passenger, to remain in total control of the vehicle. This type of training, in turn, involves a greater risk of squad car damage and officer injury. However, it has long been felt that realistic training required such speeds. For years, law enforcement brass was divided on how to best train patrol officers: high-speed training or low-speed training? The majority felt that high-speed training is the most effective method to train officers for safe, high-speed pursuits. A minority of police instructors felt that low-speed training, speeds not in excess of 35 miles per hour, which are the traditional EVOC speeds, were just as effective in training for safe, high-speed pursuits.

A 1994 test conducted by the Federal Law Enforcement Training Center (FLETC) in Glynco, Georgia, answered the question. A class of 48 federal agents going through basic training was divided in two. One of the groups was given only high-speed driver training while the other was given only low-speed training. The instructors and the

Lessons from Phoenix Police Academy

I visited the Phoenix Police Academy and was shown around the whole training area. They have maneuvers similar to what we have at The Bondurant School, including the emergency evasive maneuvers and panic stops in the accident simulator. They do four lanes wide instead of three, which is good.

During my visit, I was asked if I wanted to drive in the pursuit. Of course, I said yes! I figured it would be interesting, a lot of fun, and it would give me a firsthand chance to see the current state of the art in pursuit training.

The chief instructor asked me if I wanted to drive first. Instead, I wanted to ride first. I wanted to see the road, learn it, and see how well he handled the car, what he did, his techniques, and tactics. The Academy track is very narrow, but it's good for teaching how to stay on the road and teaching the proper line.

We took off in the violator car and the rookie officer took off behind us. He was running about 6 car lengths behind us, as he was taught. Then the driving instructor in the violator car started to pull away. In an attempt to keep up, the officer in the chase car began to make simple mistakes in the corners: braking too early or too fast, waiting too late to brake, getting a little sideways. Our chief instructor was doing a nice smooth job. We eluded the young officer by about 10 car lengths, but the recruit did a very nice job given his experience level.

Then they asked me to drive the violator car. I have been doing this type of driving for a long time. We pulled steadily away from the chase car. It wasn't very hard. However, this was against an Academy recruit. They are still learning.

Then I switched cars. I became the officer pursuing the violator. During this drill, you have to carry the microphone in your hand just as if you were calling in where you are, what you are doing, what intersection is coming up, the type of fleeing car, the license number, etc. I was chasing the chief instructor. I caught up to within two or three car lengths when he started to get a little bit ragged. I was right on line, controlling the car nice and smooth, but again, I have been driving in high-performance mode for a long time.

The chase went very well until near the end. He was trying too hard, lost it a bit, got sideways, went off the right side of the road, and took out a small street sign. I had gotten a little bit too close, about two car lengths behind him, but was watching what he was doing. I could see that he was going to lose control. He slammed on the brakes and came to an abrupt stop. So I had to brake nice and smooth, not locking the brakes up and losing control myself, which I did. I waited for him to get going again and resumed the chase.

While I was at the Academy, I observed that most recruits are doing a very nice job, but some are driving over their heads. Being chased is one thing, while doing the chasing is quite another. The one being chased will tend to overdrive the car unless he or she has been through a police or antiterrorist driving course.

During my visit to the Academy, I came to appreciate that the "hand shuffle" steering technique can work sometimes as well as the 3 and 9 hand position on the wheel. It is a different technique. I prefer the 3 and 9 position for most driving. The 3 and 9 position is a little smoother and more accurate. It is very easy with the shuffle to get the car sideways, out of shape, because you tend to turn the wheel too far and then jerk it back and forth sometimes. We saw this when we observed some of the recruits chasing the bad guy. However, it can be made to work, especially when one hand holds the radio microphone.

In a pursuit, the natural tendency is to get distracted by the siren and emergency lights. These cause a dump of adrenaline and speed up the heart rate and breathing. You have to try extra hard to concentrate. Concentrate on your own driving, while looking well ahead of the fleeing car. Don't race with the fleeing car. Don't worry about how the fleeing driver is driving his car. Drive your own car and concentrate on being smooth. Watch for his mistakes, but don't get collected in them.

I want to thank a number of members of the Phoenix Police Department for the opportunity to drive at their Academy—Officer Pat Farmer, the chief instructor who runs the Academy; Lieutenant Dave Faulkner, for assisting us in obtaining permission to attend; Officer Beth Hollick, for assisting us in obtaining permission for a ride-along; and Officer Anthony Meraz, for allowing me to ride along with him and ask questions.

—Bob Bondurant

amount of training were the same for both groups. After the training, both groups were evaluated on the same high-speed driving track. The drivers were measured by two methods: their lap time around the road racing course, and the number of driver errors or occurrences of improper driving.

The lap time for the high-speed group was 237.8 seconds versus 240.9 seconds for the low-speed group, a 1 percent difference. The high-speed group had 138 improper driving incidents compared to 101 for the low-speed group, a 37 percent difference.

The low-speed training produced safer, more conservative driving while the high-speed training produced more aggressive driving. Most significantly, this test should motivate departments that are doing no training at all because they lack high-speed training facilities. A parking lot that allows speeds up to 35 miles per hour may produce the safest police driving habits.

On a periodic basis, every 6 or 12 months, an officer needs a driving refresher. You will need a location. The location can be an abandoned airstrip, a local race track, or even a large parking lot. Consider a high school parking lot or a section of a parking lot at a large mall. Perhaps your jurisdiction includes large corporations with large parking lots. Don't let the individual parking space bumpers or parking lot light poles bother you. The course can be laid out with these in mind.

You don't have to wet down the entire track to do a low traction exercise. Just wet down the area where the police car will be driven. Bald tires and a wet track make skids and skid control easy to practice.

You want to use one of the older, higher mileage patrol cars but one that still runs well. Put a set of well-worn tires on the car to allow you to get into a slide easier. Make sure the car is in mechanically good shape. You may want to install new shocks and brakes. Be sure the oil is topped off.

Once you have the location and the training car, you need to develop a number

One of the very best training drills is a Precision Maneuvers Course. The officer must both drive and back the car through tightly spaced pylons. This teaches the officer to use all the mirrors and to know the width and length and where all four corners of the vehicle are.

The Bondurant Precision Maneuvers Course is a model for urban police departments: tight radius turns, left and right parallel parking, lock-to-lock slalom, and backing the car up hundreds of yards without hitting a pylon just six inches from the tires.

Like many departments, the Hall County, Georgia, Sheriff's Department requires deputies who drive Mustang pursuit cars to undergo additional training. Actually, all police officers and sheriff's deputies, regardless of their issue vehicle, should have periodic in-service driver training. *Dave Moon*

of simple but meaningful drills to keep your skills sharp. These may include skid control, evasive maneuvers, a precision maneuvers course, an autocross, and perhaps a mock pursuit.

Evasive Maneuver Drill

For the evasive maneuver drill, set up a course like the one at The Bondurant School.

By far the most meaningful of all in-service training exercises is the evasive maneuvers drill pioneered by Bob Bondurant. You don't need traffic lights. The instructor can flag the officer which direction to turn or simply ride along with the officer and declare the open lane . . . at the last minute, of course.

Use pylons to outline the entire approach lane and the three traffic lanes. Instead of traffic lights to indicate which lanes become suddenly blocked, you have two options. One is to have an instructor with a cone flashlight standing near the decision point. At the correct time, he can point to the left or to the right. The flashlight raised overhead can indicate to select the center lane.

The second option is to have an instructor ride as a passenger with the officer. At the correct time, the instructor can simply call out which lane to take. The advantage of this option is that the instructor can watch the hand and foot movements of the officer and help him to correct any errors. Start the drill at 25 miles per hour and increase in 5-mile per hour increments up to 45 miles per hour.

The three evasive drills should be: (1) turn into the open traffic lane and then back into the exit lane; (2) turn into the open traffic lane and then stop; (3) panic stop before entering any of the traffic lanes. A large traffic cone tied to a string can be toppled into the traffic lane to become an obstacle.

Precision Maneuvers

Another important drill is based on the Bondurant Precision Maneuvers Course. This tests the officers' ability to drive in extremely tight quarters and forces them to develop an awareness of both the car's overall width and overall length. This is an extremely relevant exercise, especially for city police departments and urban sheriffs' departments and any officer who has backed into a gas pump when coming in to refuel.

The precision maneuvers course simply duplicates normal day-to-day driving situations. The precision exercise does not train officers for life-threatening pursuits. Instead, it prepares them to avoid costly and embarrassing fender benders. It teaches them how to use their mirrors and how to shift between forward and reverse without abusing the equipment.

Precise vehicle placement literally within inches is required. The exercises can include an offset driveway pull-in, left parallel park, hard right-angle turn and back, a tight radius cul-de-sac, S-curves, and a lock-to-lock straight line slalom. Set small traffic cones just a foot wider than the squad car to mark the path.

The precision maneuvers course is also timed. Each officer has to complete the course under the time limit. When an officer completes the precision course within the time limit and without hitting any pylons by going through the course forward, the next step is to go through the course backward. Expect complaining. Only the proper use of mirrors and getting the right shoulder well up into the seat during backing will allow

The evasive maneuvers drill should include turn and drive on, turn and stop, and stop before entry. This sheriffs deputy has buried the front bumper of Bondurant's Crown Victoria without wheel lock up.

the officer to get through this very useful exercise. The precision maneuvers course teaches officers to know precisely where the four corners of their car are at all times.

The best way to learn skid control is to take an asphalt area and wet it down thoroughly. Start out slowly and build up to speed where you have control. Then set it up to have a rear-wheel skid or a front-wheel skid. The first thing you create is a front-wheel skid. If you set up a watered-down throttle steer circle, you will feel the understeer or front-wheel skid very early

Some departments, like the Portland, Oregon, Police Department, have access to a SkidCar platform large enough for a full-size cruiser.

Getting Peppered with Salt

It was the day after Christmas. The temperature was pretty low but so far, snow had been relatively light for the winter season. Because of the holidays, I was working solo on a primary beat car for that evening's third watch (4 p.m. to midnight) tour of duty and was driving one of the district's newer Chevy Caprices.

The first six hours had been nice and quiet with only a few routine disturbance calls. Right around 10 p.m. there was a radio call of an "Auto Theft Just Occurred" brief description of the car and license plate. I headed toward the location of the complainant to write the report. As I approached a stop sign, a car matching the wanted vehicle went through the intersection. As I strained to catch a glimpse of the rear plate, the dispatcher said, "All units stand by as we change shifts."

That is the worst time of the tour of duty—when one dispatcher is leaving and the oncoming crew sits down and plugs in to begin their night. Although it seems like five minutes, the momentary lapse of communication lasts only a few seconds. I repeated "2424. What's the plate number on that stolen car?" By the third request, the new dispatcher familiarized himself with the incident and repeated the license number. A look at the rear of the car in front of me confirmed it.

"2424. I'm sitting at a red light behind that car right now. Southbound on Rogers at Clark Street. One male occupant." The light changed to green, and the car turned north onto Clark Street. With a block to go to the city limits, I wanted to at least attempt to the curb the car in Chicago. According to the radio, the first backup unit was less than a block away. My attention was focused on the car in front of me. As I flipped on my blue lights, the stolen car accelerated but, to my surprise, turned east on Howard Street and headed toward the nearby CTA bus terminal. I managed to stay a safe distance behind him while driving, keeping an eye on traffic, and talking on the radio at the same time.

As two assisting units converged on the exit to the bus terminal from opposite directions, the stolen car managed to snake between them like thread through the tiny eye of a needle. I was forced to slow down a bit, but still maintained visual contact with the vehicle as the driver finished his loop which put him right back to where the pursuit had begun. This time around, the offender killed the car's lights and sped north over the border into Evanston, which had no overhead street lighting on that block. About two blocks into Evanston, there is a set of railroad tracks that bridge across the road diagonally. The road makes a quick right-then-left jog, to pass under the tracks at a right angle.

The street looked like it was glistening as my blue strobes and flashing headlights lit the pavement in front of me. The fleeing sedan was kicking dust, and my squad car sounded like I was driving on a gravel road. I soon figured out that this was excess road salt, lots and lots of it. The driver of the stolen car soon discovered this too as he bolted toward the railroad underpass. Through the dust, I saw brake lights and sparks as the stolen car struck the concrete pylons and came to rest sideways, smoking and blocking my path. The driver bailed out to flee on foot. I was closing in fast—about a millisecond to slam on the brakes and hope for the best.

In an automobile built before anti-lock brakes, pumping the pedal was about your only hope. The effort was futile. The large amount of salt on the roadway afforded my car no controlled braking power at all and it slammed head-on into the center concrete abutment. With the bridge being slightly angled, the squad car was pushed to the right, careened off the abandoned stolen car, and continued through the underpass, right toward the fleeing offender. I pushed the car to continue, but it went about as far as it would go. The crushed fender had locked up the left front wheel, and the front clip was shifted about a foot to the right.

The offender was captured immediately and charged with a felony. The crumbled, smoking remnants of the victim's car were returned, and the four-month-old squad car was patched up to look as good as new, although it never did drive quite right after that.

—*Officer Greg Reynolds*
Chicago Police Department

on. The only way you're going to get out of a front-wheel skid is to pump the brakes on and off or activate the ABS to regain traction. With traction on the front wheels, you will be out of the front-wheel skid.

Autocross as Training

An autocross is excellent training. An autocross is like a small road course except you mark the course, or just the corners, with pylons. The autocross is a handling course with both tight and wide, left- and right-hand turns, and short straights. The autocross can be timed. The path is laid out between sets of cones the officer must drive between. The cone spacing can be open, allowing more freedom in negotiating through the course, or it can be quite tight with little leeway.

The autocross utilizes all the various driving skills. The best times come from drivers who scrub off the least speed during cornering, spin the wheels the least during acceleration, and slide the tires the least during braking. The best times come from drivers who control their aggression.

Sportscar clubs across the country host autocross competitions on parking lots, abandoned air strips, and small race tracks. The speeds are kept low by designing the layout fairly tight. The speed on most parking lot courses is under 40 miles per hour, while the race tracks are typically limited by a pylon chicane to speeds under 65 miles per hour. The autocross is just like the EVOC course taught at most police academies. Vehicle control, not sheer speed, is the goal. It is basically a precision maneuvers course that forces the officer to drive through a complex line involving heavy braking, short bursts of acceleration, and tight turns.

The autocross has a number of advantages for police training. The precision driving and relatively low speeds are typical of a city pursuit. The duration of most autocross courses is 1 1/2 to 3 minutes. The average pursuit lasts 3 minutes. The autocross and the city pursuit both involve intense, heart-pounding, shortness-of-breath driving. It may be helpful to join a car club that autocrosses because the club will have organized, periodic events that someone else has already set-up and coordinated.

Two groups of agents undergoing training at the Federal Law Enforcement Training Center were put to a driving test on this flat track. The group that received only low-speed, EVOC-style training was nearly as fast around the track as the group that received only high-speed, race track-style training. The EVOC group, however, drove much safer.

They don't call an autocross a "sea of cones" for no reason. The autocross is a specific course, laid out by cones, that allows the officer some freedom to chose his line around the course. The autocross taxes nearly all driving skills.

The legwork is done. Insurance and liability are already covered at the event site. All the officer has to do is show up and drive. Events are held throughout the year in every major city.

The autocross is a sport designed for cars that are driven every day to work. Wear and tear on the vehicle is minimal. While

The best times on an autocross course come from controlling your aggression, avoiding wheelspin, tire scrubbing, and skidding. Police officers can hone their vehicle control skills while having someone else do all the organizational work. Simply attend an autocross hosted by a local sports car club. Don't forget to activate the lightbar during your timed run! *Dave Scott*

EVOC courses prepare the officer for low and medium speed problems. The way a car reacts at speeds over 100 mph can only be felt while actually driving at those speeds. The Hall County, Georgia, Sheriffs Department puts their fleet of DUI Task Force Mustangs to work at Road Atlanta. *Dave Moon*

each event has race-prepared classes, the vast majority of autocross cars are simply driven home and then to work. The shocks, tires, and brake pads do not need to be replaced before and after the autocross as they do on the high-speed, race-track style of training.

Two problems exist with this training concept. The first is gaining acceptance from the police administration to take a government-owned police vehicle to a "race." One aspect is the image. The other is the fear of wear and tear. The image question is simply a matter of emphasizing the training aspect. The wear and tear question may be resolved by using "pool" or older cruisers until the minimal wear is confirmed.

The second issue is getting officers to show up. The officer in a full-size sedan will be clearly outrun by a bunch of Mustangs, Camaros, Firebirds and every kind of sports car, many with less power than the police cruiser. The reality is the full-size police sedan will come in dead last. Last in class. Slowest overall. Most cops are not used to being outrun, coming in last, or beaten fair and square. The solution, of course, is for the cops to do what they always do: show up en masse to support one another. You won't be competing against those pesky Mustangs and Camaros. You will be running against one another. Give the event organizers a heads-up that a half-dozen cops are coming. You may even be able to persuade the competition director to open up the pylon spacing enough to get your Crown Vics through. A big difference exists for a course laid out for a Mazda Miata or even a Mustang and a course laid out for a full-size, four-door sedan.

Be prepared to get in the spirit of the autocross: turn on your emergency lights as you make the run. The crowd of sports car drivers will expect it!

Appendix A

The Nine Ts of Pursuit Driving

An analysis of actual pursuits shows the major reason many of them turn out badly is not the officers' lack of driving skills, but rather their failure to apply these skills properly. The 9T approach to pursuit driving attempts to assist police officers in the key decisions of whether to pursue or not and how to pursue.

1. Think

Think about pursuits from all points of view: the officer, the suspect, and the innocent third parties. This should be done both prior to and during the pursuit.

Offenders believe that they can outrun the police or that if they go beyond jurisdictional limits, the police will end the chase. When it becomes apparent that the fleeing suspect shows no inclination to stop, officers should consider other alternatives, such as properly establishing a roadblock or abandoning the pursuit. The option to terminate often leads officers to believe that if one gets away, the violator and others will look at this as encouragement to continue the behavior. While this possibility exists, their immediate obligation is to ensure the safety of the public. That responsibility rests with law enforcement. Police officers need to resist the temptation to duplicate the immature behavior of those whom they pursue.

Think about the innocent third parties. From accounts given by these individuals, most third parties had no warning prior to being struck either by the offender or the police. In other words, either they simply failed to hear the sirens or see the lights, or they didn't have time to react to them.

Officers often fail to plan ahead and warn others in the path of the vehicles involved. Or, they simply lose sight of the fact that the public legally shares space with them. Remember, officers must request the right of way. They cannot demand it. Only the motoring public can grant it.

2. Talk

Talk about pursuits one on one, in group discussions, or by exchanging written communications, thereby constructively evaluating pursuit alternatives.

Numerous articles in professional journals recommend that all pursuit policies should include a mandatory review and critique after each pursuit. Too many times, department administrators consider pursuits successful when officers apprehend the suspect and no accidents, injuries, or fatalities occur. Yet, each pursuit offers the department a prime opportunity to learn, because the pursuit presents a real-world example for those involved to critique the pursuit.

If administrators constructively evaluate each pursuit, they would find areas of vulnerability that could be improved or eliminated. Disseminating the results of the evaluations not only reinforces appropriate pursuit behavior but also points out shortcomings and potential hazards. Such communications protect the officers and their departments in the event of future pursuits and possibly prevent a tragic experience for all involved.

3. Track

Track pursuits and use resulting data as a basis for training and formulating a pursuit policy.

Many departments fail to keep data on pursuits for fear of media exploitation or the possibility of enhancing a plaintiff's claim in a lawsuit. However, some departments see the value in compiling pursuit statistics. Agencies that maintain information on pursuits conducted by their personnel believe it is more important to rely on what really happened than to react to media sensationalism or the presumptions of the plaintiff's attorneys.

The California Highway Patrol uses the information compiled to justify one of the most comprehensive driving programs in the nation. Its critique of every pursuit allows the department to identify those officers who need to be retrained and to communicate problems to all employees, in order to minimize the danger to the public.

In 1988, the Utah Department of Public Safety conducted a survey of State law enforcement agencies to determine the number of officers involved in pursuits, the average duration of pursuits, and the number of accidents that resulted. The information obtained showed a majority of the accidents, and the injuries and deaths that subsequently occurred, could have been prevented with more adequate training.

Data on pursuits and emergency response can educate decision makers as to what is really happening. Such information can substantiate current policies and practices regarding driver training or inspire departments to institute better training programs and pursuit policies.

4. Tailor

Tailor a clear set of written guidelines and then use the guidelines to protect the officer, the department, and the public.

In today's litigious society, it is amazing to find that many law enforcement agencies do not have a pursuit policy, and among those that do, the policies are often ambiguous and misleading. Officers involved in pursuits must correctly understand the interpretation of the words "reasonable," "due regard," and "good judgment." Police pursuit policies should include legal authorization for pursuits, continuation and termination factors, and detailed responsibilities for support units, supervisors, and communications personnel. The policies must also cover permissible vehicle tactics, pursuit activities in other jurisdictions, reviews of pursuit activities, and training requirements.

5. Train

Train all officers on when and how to initiate and terminate a pursuit.

With the 1989 Supreme Court decision in City of Canton v. Harris, it becomes increasingly apparent that law enforcement administrators are under the scrutiny of legal precedent to provide training in the duties that are a condition of employment. Failure to do so would be considered "deliberately indifferent to the rights of citizens with whom officers will likely have contact." The Supreme Court's decision means that if an officer is going to engage in such an activity as a pursuit, then that officer must be given some training on how to carry out that responsibility.

Pursuit driving requires specific skills and abilities not easily taught on neighborhood streets and interstate highways. Fortunately, these skills can be acquired without the use of an expensive facility or equipment.

6. Toughen

Toughen laws to make eluding or evading the police an offense equal to or greater than driving under the influence.

Recently, the State of New Jersey enacted laws designed to deter motorists from fleeing a police officer. The laws stipulate that a motorist found guilty will have his or her driver's license suspended for six months to two years.

Motorists who do not have valid driver's licenses may be imprisoned for 90 days for a first offense, 6 months for a second offense, and 1 year for any subsequent offense. The laws also provide for up to 18 months in prison and a $7,500 fine for licensed drivers. In addition, the laws include a refutable inference that the owner of the motor vehicle was the vehicle's operator at the time of the pursuit.

Fortunately, other states are examining the possibility of enacting laws similar to those in New Jersey to create a deterrent for the potential pursuit offender. The New Jersey laws, or the Utah law that makes evading the police a felony in most circumstances, send a clear message that the public and law enforcement will no longer tolerate any individual who jeopardizes the safety of others by engaging in conduct that threatens the well-being of the officer or innocent third parties.

7. Technology

Technology such as video interaction and reflecting license plates should be used where possible.

Commercially available pursuit simulators and model boards offer financially feasible electronic training enhancement. These simulation devices provide an alternative means of training in the practical application of driving principles taught in the classroom. The ability to put officers in pursuit situations in which instructors or supervisors could monitor their reactions to changing and unexpected scenarios makes simulation an attractive alternative. Simulations, like FATS for handguns, allow for scenarios considered too dangerous to conduct on a driving course; the consequences of a simulated roll-over or collision are restricted to a classroom environment.

Reflecting license plates illuminate the plate and enhance an officer's ability to confirm ownership without being extremely close to the vehicle. These plates help officers to determine whether the pursued vehicle has been stolen, to establish ownership, or to determine the possible criminal involvement of the owner or driver. In cases where there is a rebuttable inference law, such as the one in New Jersey, the officer maintains the option to terminate the pursuit in some cases and to employ enforcement proceedings at a later time.

8. Televise

Attempt to work with the print and electronic media to be more responsible in portraying high-speed chases. Also, make public service announcements to remind citizens of the seriousness of evading the police. After spending years watching television or going to the movies, impressionable police recruits enter driver training programs without a realistic perspective on how to handle an emergency response, let alone a high-speed pursuit. Without proper training, supervision, and modification of unrefined behavior, law enforcement administrators can expect reenactments of Hollywood's version of police pursuits in a real-world environment. When officers engage in tactics that they perceive necessary to stop a violator, the tactics should reflect proper training, not the latest movie release.

Public service announcements, similar to the advertising sponsored by many states against drunk drivers and against aggressive drivers, provide another means to make people aware of the dangers involved in fleeing the police. Perhaps an emphatic antiflee campaign, broadcasting the hazards and ultimate consequences, would also deter motorists from trying to escape the police while in their vehicles.

9. Terminate

Terminate as many pursuits as possible. By implementing the previous eight suggestions, the number of pursuits will likely decrease. Although there will always be some situations requiring pursuit, as many as 50 percent of present pursuits might be eliminated through comprehensive training, the development of specific policies and procedures, and keener awareness of the outcome of pursuits.

Reprinted with permission of Earl R. Morris.

Appendix B

About the Authors

Bob Bondurant

In 2000, Bob Bondurant celebrated 32 years of professional driving instruction. Internationally recognized as the leading authority on cutting-edge driving techniques, Bondurant is the dean of advanced driving instructors. While other driving schools have popped up over the years, The Bondurant School of High Performance Driving remains the most prestigious driving school in the world.

Over 80,000 students have learned from Bondurant's experience and expertise. These include race car drivers, housewives, celebrities, VIP chauffeurs, teenagers, movie and television stars, factory workers, businessmen, and Hollywood stunt drivers. Celebrities he has taught include Tim Allen, Clint Eastwood, Paul Newman. Bruce Jenner, Gabrielle Reece, Candice Bergen, Gene Hackman, Crystal Bernard, Lee Majors, James Garner, Lorenzo Lamas, David Hasselhoff, and William Shatner. Now famous race car drivers who have had Bob Bondurant as their instructor include Al Unser, Jr., Bill Elliott, Scott Pruett, Dale Jarrett, Kyle Petty, Dale Earnhardt, Mark Martin, Jeff Gordon, Bobby LaBonte, Rick Mears, and Tony Stewart.

Of course, Bondurant has also trained a wide variety of police officers, sheriffs' deputies, state troopers, and highway patrolmen from all over the country. His training segments on emergency driving have appeared in police magazines like Law and Order and on the Law Enforcement Television Network (LETN). Police departments he has trained include: Alaska State Troopers; Jordan Police Department, country of Jordan; Los Angeles, California, Police Department; Los Angeles County, California, Sheriff's Office; Maricopa County, Arizona, Sheriff's Office; Oakland, California, Police Department; Ontario, California, Police Department; San Francisco, California, Police Department; San Mateo, California, Police Department; Santa Ana, California, Police Department; Santa Rosa, California,

Bob Bondurant is an internationally recognized driving instructor and has been for more than 30 years. Police departments he has instructed over the years include Los Angeles Police, Los Angeles County Sheriff, San Francisco Police, Maricopa County, Arizona Sheriff, and Alaska State Troopers. Rick Scuteri

Bob Bondurant raced Corvettes in southern California in the late 1950s, and in 1963 joined the Carroll Shelby Ford Cobra team. In 1964, Bondurant, and co-driver Dan Gurney, won the GT class in the 24 Hours of LeMans in this Cobra Daytona Coupe. In 1965, driving a Cobra Daytona Coupe, Bondurant won eight out of ten endurance races helping Shelby American win the World Manufacturer's Championship for Ford by beating Ferrari for the first time. Bernard Cahier

Sheriff's Department; and various other government agencies.

Bob Bondurant began his racing career with an Indian Scout motorcycle on local dirt ovals in southern California at the age of 18. His first race car was a Morgan Plus 4, which he campaigned in 1956. By 1958, he had worked his way up to racing Corvettes. The next year, he won 18 of 20 races and the West Coast "B" Production Championship. Valvoline named him the 1959 Corvette Driver of the Year. In 1959, he was once again the Sports Car Club of America (SCCA) B Production Championship winner.

In 1963, Bondurant joined Carroll Shelby's Ford Cobra team and the next year he won the GT Class Championship at the 24 Hours of LeMans along with co-driver Dan Gurney. They ended up fourth overall, first in GT, in their Ford Cobra Daytona Coupe.

In 1965, Bondurant repeated his GT Championship, and won 8 out of 10 races. These races included GT class wins at the Sebring 12-hour endurance race, and the 1,000 Kilometer races at Rheims, Spa, and Nurburgring race. Bondurant helped Shelby American to win the World Manufacturers' Championship for Ford in 1965, driving a Ford Cobra Daytona coupe, beating Ferrari for the very first time.

Also in 1965, Bondurant set the lap record at Monaco driving a BMC-powered Cooper Formula 3 car for Ken Tyrell. That same year, he won at Monza in a Lotus F3 car. At the end of the same year, he drove a Formula 2 car for Tim Parnell at Rheims,

France and raced two races for Ken Tyrell in a Formula 2 BRM. He also drove a Formula 2 car for Team Lotus and Ron Harris at Coppa Acerbo, Sicily. Bondurant then went on to Formula 1 cars, racing for Ferrari at the U.S. Grand Prix at Watkins Glen and a Formula 1 Lotus for Tim Parnell at the Mexican Grand Prix. In 1966, Bondurant drove an ex-BRM factory F1 car for Bernard White Racing and placed fourth at the Monaco Grand Prix. He continued the season through Monza. For the U.S. and Mexican Grand Prix, Bob moved on to drive for Dan Gurney's All American Racers F1 Eagle Team. He also drove for Ferrari in 1966, campaigning GT prototypes at all of the long distance races.

While racing in Europe in 1966, Bondurant served as a technical consultant and drove the camera car for John Frankenheimer's epic racing movie, Grand Prix. Among the highlights of working on the film, Bondurant was responsible for training James Garner, Yves Montand, Antonio Sabato, and Brian Bedford for their driving roles. Working on the film had a great side benefit. Bondurant was able to drive every Grand Prix road course on the circuit for two weeks before and after every Formula 1 race. He would come to know well the great road racing courses of the world.

In 1967, Bondurant joined with Peter Revson (of the Revlon family) to drive Can-Am race cars for the Dana Chevrolet team. Can-Am and the United States Road Racing Championship were growing in popularity about this time.

Later in the year, while driving in a USRRC race in a Can-Am car at Watkins Glen, Bondurant suffered a life-threatening accident. The steering arm broke on his McLaren MkII Chevrolet. Bondurant hit a dirt embankment at 150 miles per hour. His McLaren rolled end over end eight times. Bondurant broke both ankles, a thigh bone, several ribs, and chipped a vertebra in his back. It took him three years to fully recover.

While recovering in the hospital, Bondurant contemplated his future. He had enjoyed his experiences coaching the actors for *Grand Prix,* and as a substitute for Pete Brock (of Datsun 240Z racing fame) at Carroll Shelby's Driving School at Riverside Raceway. He also enjoyed teaching at a number of SCCA racing schools. During this recovery period he formulated plans for a driving school. If he had the physical ability, he would take his expert knowledge and experience of driving and start a school to teach others. His plans were to rehabilitate himself while conducting the School.

On February 14, 1968, Bondurant officially opened the doors of The Bob Bondurant School of High Performance Driving. The School was based at the Orange County International Raceway near Los Angeles. His first school cars were three Datsuns, a

Lola T-70 Can-Am car, and an open-wheel Formula Vee. The first week he had three students.

The second week he had just two students. However, the two were Paul Newman and Robert Wagner, who were training for the movie, *Winning.* As technical advisor for the film, Bondurant taught the actors and drove the camera car, just as he had for *Grand Prix.* In 1970, The Bondurant School moved to nearby Ontario Motor Speedway. This was also the year that Bondurant returned to Can-Am racing. He finished second at the Can-Am race at Road America. In 1971, he continued his Can-Am effort and finished fourth at Mosport Park.

After the 1972 season, Bondurant retired from the racing circuit to devote full time to the School. In 1973, the School moved to the Sears Point International Raceway in rolling northern California, near Sonoma. In 1983, Ford Motor Company became involved as a sponsor of The Bondurant School. Ford provides technical support and vehicles. In turn, The Bondurant School became one of Ford's most important proving grounds.

In March 1990, Bondurant's dream of his own state-of-the-art driver training facility came true. Bondurant is a licensed airplane and helicopter pilot. However, for his dream, he also

In early 1965, Bob Bondurant drove a Formula 3 open-wheel Cooper racer for Ken Tyrrell and set a track record at Monaco. Later that year, Bondurant moved up to the ultimate ride: this Ferrari factory Formula 1 race car. Bondurant raced Formula 1 cars in 1965 and 1966.

That's Bob Bondurant, Ron Rondel, and James Garner during filming of the 1966 movie, Grand Prix. *Bondurant trained Garner, Yves Montand, Antonio Sabato, and Brian Bedford for their driving roles. In addition to training actors for the movie, Bondurant served as their technical consultant and also drove the camera car for the film.*

learned how to drive a bulldozer so he could help build the 1.3 to 1.6-mile racing course used by the School. This is the only full-size road racing course ever built specifically for training. It has every kind of curve and camber a racer or driver will ever encounter on a track or on the street. A 8-acre asphalt pad is the home of the Throttle Steer Circle, Handling Oval, Accident Avoidance Simulator, Slalom Course, Autocross and Skid Pad. Today, The Bondurant School maintains a fleet of over 150 Jack Roush-prepared Ford vehicles, including Formula Ford race cars, Mustang Cobra R and Mustang GT student cars, and the latest version of the Crown Victoria Police Interceptors for law enforcement students, as well as more than 30 of Bondurant's F1-style Formula Fords.

The Crown Victoria training cars are specially prepared for Bondurant by Jack Roush Racing. They have a six-point integral safety cage, four-point racing-style seat belts, a safety fuel cell, and a toggle switch-activated, halon fire suppression system. Each is fitted with NASCAR style window nets. The cable-controlled emergency brake is replaced with a special hydraulic brake system to allow forward 180 degree spins. These police cruisers are also used by students in the Executive Protection/Antikidnapping Course.

Bondurant remains a consumer advisor and spokesman for Ford. He travels the country promoting safe and advanced driving skills. He was recently featured on the Ford ABS brake video, which was sent to every police department in America. He talks with Ford dealers about selling high-performance vehicles and to consumer groups about safe driving. Bondurant also advises Ford engineers on the handling and performance characteristics of future cars. Bondurant has served as an expert witness on automotive issues for Ford, Pontiac, Jeep, and Volkswagen. Bondurant continues to race in a few, select vintage and historic automobile races. He is typically behind the wheel of a Shelby Cobra or a Formula 1 car.

Bob Bondurant suffered a serious crash driving a Can-Am car in 1967. During his recovery, he formulated the plans for his driving school. In 1968, he opened the Bob Bondurant School of High Performance Driving in Orange County, CA. Two of the first students at The Bondurant School were Paul Newman, right, and Robert Wagner. The two actors were training for the 1968 movie, Winning. *Bondurant, left, served as technical consultant and drove the camera car during filming.*

Bondurant is the author of the book *Defensive Driving,* (Motorbooks International, 1975) and coauthor with John Blakemore of *Bob Bondurant on High Performance Driving* (Motorbooks, 1982).

The Jordan Program

While The Bondurant School of High Performance Driving is primarily known in the United States, it has conducted programs all over the world. Earlier this year when Bob was at the Monaco Grand Prix he saw some familiar faces from the Ford Motor Company division in the country of Jordan. They asked if he would be interested in training their police personnel who had just received 100 new Crown Victoria police Interceptors. He accepted the invitation and with two of his instructors conducted a program at the military airport in Amman, Jordan.

The School modified their regular police training to address their special needs. Pursuits and daily police driving appear to be a little more aggressive in that part of the world. The School taught the anti-kidnapping and terrorist driving maneuvers including ramming and take-outs as well as forward and reverse 180s. The 12 students included the top police instructors from the Jordan area—2 of the students were security officials for Jordan and 1 was from Palace security. Out of 12 students only 4 spoke fluent English and they served as interpreters. In four days The School not only taught them our program, but also how to train their other officers these invaluable techniques.

If you're interested in conducting a program please contact The Bondurant School of High Performance Driving and they will be happy to customize one to suit your needs.

Corporal Ed Sanow

Corporal Ed Sanow of the Benton County, Indiana, Sheriff's Department raced a Ford Galaxie on dirt ovals in Ohio before he had a driver's license. During his college days, Sanow was the competition director for the Purdue University Auto Club. He finished seventh in the nation at the 1976 SCCA Solo I championships in an A/Sedan Mustang. Sanow raced an A/Sports Racing Mustang at SCCA Regional road racing events in the Midwest.

Sanow was a student in the first Bondurant Police Instructor course held at the Firebird Raceway. Sanow is a contributing editor on police vehicles and other law enforcement subjects for *Law and Order* and *Law Enforcement Technology* magazines. His articles on police enforcement and pursuit driving have also appeared in *Police* magazine. He is the author of six books on police cars. Sanow is one of the most active traffic enforcement officers in his county. His patrol cars have included the LT1 Camaro, LT1 Caprice, and the SOHC Crown Victoria.

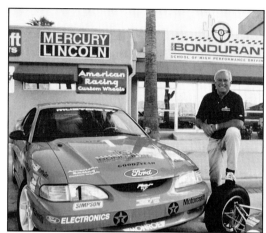

In 1990, Bob Bondurant's dream of creating a state-of-the-art personal driving facility came true. Bondurant designed the 1.6 mile road racing course, which has every kind of curve and camber a racer or driver will ever find on a track or on the street. Called "The Bondurant School" it is situated near Phoenix, Arizona, and includes courses for all age and driving groups. The school maintains a fleet of more than 150 vehicles including SVT Ford Mustang Cobra Rs, Formula Fords, Mustang Cobras, Formula Fords, Mustnag GTs, and Crown Victoria "Police Interceptors." Rick Scuteri

Cpl. Ed Sanow, with the Benton County, IN Sheriffs Department, is a contributing editor to Law *and* Order *and* Law Enforcement Technology *magazines. An active traffic enforcement officer, Sanow is the author of numerous books on vintage and modern police cars.*

Index